Contents

List of illustrations		vi
Foreword		ix
Acknowledgements		xii
Introduction		xiv
1	Is alcohol education needed? How should it be done?	1
2	The research	31
3	The baseline survey	41
4	The teaching package	60
5	Comments from the classroom: what the teachers and pupils thought	71
6	Was the alcohol education effective?	83
7	Conclusions and implications	95
	Appendix 1a Alcohol education follow-up questionnaire	109
	Appendix 1b Addsyg ar alcohol ail holiadur	135
	Appendix 2 Statistical analyses used in evaluation study	160
	Bibliography	162
	Index	168

Illustrations

FIGURES

1.1	The epidemiological triangle	14
2.1	Map of Britain to show the position of three regions selected for study	34
2.2	Detailed research design	36
3.1	Quantity consumed on last occasion	43
3.2	Maximum consumption for study group	44
3.3a	Sex differences in beer consumption	49
3.3b	Sex differences in wine consumption	49
3.3c	Sex differences in maximum consumption	50
3.4	Sex differences in frequency of consumption	50
3.5	Sex differences in current tobacco use	53
A.1	Three-by-three factorial model	160

TABLES

1.1	UK consumption of alcohol	3
1.2	Alcohol consumption per head in leading countries	4
2.1	Unemployment rate by local authority districts at time of surveys	33
2.2	Regional distribution of age and sex	38
3.1	Illicit drug use for total sample	47
3.2	Effects of alcohol consumption more likely to have been experienced by males	52

6.1	Experience of alcohol – before and after the educational intervention	85
6.2	Average scores on knowledge quiz – before and after the alcohol education	86
6.3	Knowledge items influenced by intervention	88
6.4	Attitude change by group	89
6.5	Alcohol-related behaviour changes following the educational intervention	91

Foreword

During the 1960s and 1970s alcohol consumption levels increased enormously in many countries. This was accompanied by a disturbing increase in alcohol-related problems including those involving young people. During the past decade there has been a considerable international variation in alcohol consumption levels. In some countries, such as France, these have declined. Elsewhere, such as Australia, Canada, New Zealand, the UK and the USA alcohol consumption has remained relatively stable or has risen only slowly.

'Alcohol misuse' or 'alcohol-related problems' encompass a wide range of adverse consequences somehow connected with the inappropriate or deleterious use of alcohol. These problems may be due to prolonged heavy drinking and involve alcohol dependence or, more commonly, be due to intermittent heavy drinking or even a single episode of heavy drinking. The consumption of alcohol is implicated in a daunting array of problems. These include illness, death, public order offences, and a host of social, family and occupational problems. In most countries alcohol is popular and widely used. Its use in moderation is normally harmless and may in certain respects be beneficial. Even so ethyl alcohol is a psychoactive (mind-altering) depressant drug. Its use is associated with disinhibition and the slowing of the central nervous system. Accordingly, alcohol may very easily be misused, sometimes with tragic consequences.

Public concern frequently becomes focused upon alcohol misuse amongst young people. The mass media often exaggerate or distort this phenomenon. Nevertheless, in many countries youthful alcohol misuse is well established as a serious problem. This is reflected by public order offences, drunken driving and in some localities, an increase in young men and women developing chronic alcohol problems. The tragedy of young people suffering or inflicting trauma, injury or death through the misuse of alcohol heightens the importance of devising strategies to curb alcohol misuse. The young are often regarded as being high priority targets for alcohol education. This is for two reasons. First, young people are commonly perceived as being especially vulnerable to alcohol misuse due to their inexperience. Second, it is sometimes hoped that if youthful drinking habits could be influenced for the better this might provide a degree of protection both in the short term and later in life.

Abundant evidence supports the conclusion that alcohol consumption is *associated* with many types of problem. Even so, the precise causal contribution of alcohol to any specific problem is often unclear. For example, many of those convicted of violent crime have been reported to have been 'under the influence' of alcohol at the time of the offence. In spite of this it is invariably not possible to determine the extent to which drinking may have precipitated any specific criminal event. It is emphasised that the effects of any drug depend upon an interaction between the substance in question, the characteristics of the user and the environment in which use occurs. The consequences of drinking alcohol are strongly influenced by social and cultural factors as well as by economic conditions.

Overall levels of 'alcohol misuse' such as alcohol-related illnesses, deaths and crimes are clearly linked to the rise and fall in general national levels of alcohol consumption. Accordingly, attempts to curb alcohol misuse face major social and political problems. The American experience of prohibition and the recent attempt in the USSR to reduce alcohol production, and thereby consumption, both failed because they lacked popular support. Strategies to reduce alcohol misuse have to operate within the framework of what is politically acceptable. The ideal solution for alcohol misuse would be if health education could successfully 'insulate' people from the risks of misuse or harmful drinking. Health education is important and is also popular. Sadly, in many areas health education has not been very successful in leading people to change their behaviour. So far evidence suggests that if there is a 'magic bullet' with which to banish alcohol misuse from the face of the globe it is not health education.

People drink for many complex, varied and often contradictory reasons. It is therefore unrealistic to expect even the most painstaking and elaborate programme of health education to counter these. Accordingly, past experience suggests that the gains to be made from alcohol education may inevitably be modest ones. This fact was the starting point of the endeavour described in this book.

Gellisse Bagnall is a psychologist with a background of research into education as well as in alcohol epidemiology. She embarked upon an initiative designed to investigate whether or not it was possible to provide alcohol education for teenagers which has *tangible* positive results. Her study was undertaken in full awareness of the ineffective and sometimes even counterproductive nature of many past experiments in alcohol education. The depressing track record of alcohol education had to be reconciled with the need to produce an approach that fitted into current classroom conditions and which appealed not only to teenagers but also to their teachers. Accordingly, Gellisse Bagnall sought the active involvement of teachers in England, Wales and Scotland in not only the implementation, but also the basic design, of her alcohol education materials. It was frankly acknowledged that alcohol education is only a rudimentary science, with no proven technology. Because of this Gellisse adopted a suitably sceptical approach to her educational materials. These were tested under controlled conditions.

This book describes an experiment in practical classroom alcohol education. It also describes the changing use of alcohol, tobacco and illicit drugs in a study group of British teenagers. Gellisse Bagnall is to be congratulated for the painstaking manner in which she conducted a difficult study and for the lucid manner in which she describes it. She has produced an important and realistic overview of the status of alcohol education as well as demonstrating that alcohol education can produce pleasing results.

Martin Plant
Director
Alcohol Research Group
University of Edinburgh
February 1990

Acknowledgements

The research project on which this book is based was funded jointly by the Alcohol Education and Research Council and the Brewers' Society, with additional support from the Scotch Whisky Association. Further sponsorship from the Brewers' Society made it possible to publish the end product of the research, an alcohol education package, at a price which schools could afford.

The fieldwork for this project was totally dependent on the goodwill of local education authorities and schools which agreed to participate in the research. I am extremely grateful for the willing co-operation which prevailed throughout the study. The research phase would have been much less enjoyable without the welcome extended to me and my colleagues from all teachers involved, despite the disruption to their timetable caused by a large-scale survey. Additional thanks must go to the teachers who worked with me to develop the alcohol education materials, and to the 1,560 pupils who so willingly answered the survey questions.

Throughout the duration of the research and the writing of this book, I have received help and encouragement from many colleagues and friends. Although too numerous to name here, my thanks must go to all of them. Special mention, however, must be made of some particular sources of support. Firstly all my colleagues in the Alcohol Research Group at Edinburgh University, past and present, must be thanked for putting up with me, especially when I have been under pressure. I am also grateful to John Duffy and Ian Young for commenting on individual chapters. Particular thanks must go to Martin Plant and Dave Peck, who were joint grant-holders during the research phase, and who continue as joint supervisors of my doctoral dissertation on this research. I am especially grateful to Martin Plant for his encouragement in the preparation of this book, and for his contribution in the Foreword. I am indebted to all the Alcohol Research Group secretaries for their assistance, but especially to Sheila McLennan who typed the manuscript with great care and efficiency.

My final acknowledgement must go to my family, especially my husband Ron, without whose understanding and support this book is unlikely to have been completed.

Gellisse Bagnall
Alcohol Research Group
Department of Psychiatry
University of Edinburgh
February 1990

Introduction

GENERAL OVERVIEW

Alcohol and its mind-altering qualities have been enjoyed by human societies throughout the world for centuries. This is acknowledged in the Bible: 'Give strong drink to him who is perishing, and wine to those in bitter distress: let them drink and forget their poverty and remember their misery no more' (Proverbs 31: 4–7). At the same time, however, the less acceptable face of alcohol use has been recognised, and appropriate 'warnings' issued for the benefit of those who overindulge: 'Wine is a mocker, stronger drink a brawler; and whoever is led astray by it is not wise' (Proverbs 20: 1).

The pessimist might agree that little has changed over time, with the 'scourge' of alcohol misuse still prevalent despite enormous progress in medical knowledge, educational techniques and general public awareness of health-related issues. It is beyond the capabilities of this book to dispel such doubt completely. On the other hand, it is hoped that the reader will find a balanced view of the current status of strategies for preventing alcohol misuse. In particular the book will argue that school-based alcohol education has an important and effective role to play in curbing alcohol misuse.

The contribution of education in the context of psychoactive substance use has been noted by Plant *et al.*:

> Education is important. It is important as a symbolic statement that society is concerned about alcohol, tobacco and illicit drug problems. It is important that available knowledge should be disseminated as widely as possible. Young people, the population at large, those in the 'helping professions', journalists and politicians are all legitimate and important target groups for health education.
> (Plant, *et al.* 1985: 119)

Discussions on the prevention of alcohol misuse inevitably highlight the role of education, all too often heralded as an obvious panacea to all society's ills. The term 'alcohol education' means different things to different people. To some it refers to *primary prevention*, or stopping people from ever developing problems which relate to alcohol consumption. To others, especially clinicians, it may be interpreted in terms of *secondary prevention*, or arresting misuse which already exists before it becomes chronic or seriously incapacitating. No single programme is likely to be able to meet all needs and expectations. Rather the nature of any alcohol educational initiative should be determined by a clear knowledge of the people for whom it is intended. This in turn will indicate the most appropriate educational strategy or approach.

SCHOOL-BASED ALCOHOL EDUCATION

At the time of writing, the topic of alcohol education generally receives very low priority in the school curriculum in Britain and many other countries. Although some schools have developed their own alcohol education, many others appear to have given little consideration to the topic. Such diversity of provision results largely from the difficulty of slotting health education or alcohol education into the curriculum. As with all other subjects which are not compulsory or formally assessed, school-based alcohol education has to compete for space with other topics in an already well-filled curriculum. The low priority apparently given to alcohol education in this respect cannot be fully explained in terms of poor resources. Some excellent alcohol education materials are available to schools throughout the United Kingdom. These include an alcohol education pack for 11- to 16-year-olds published jointly in 1984 by the Teachers Advisory Council on Alcohol and Drug Education and the Health Education Council. Alcohol is also a topic in the health education programme for 13- to 18-year-olds produced in 1984 by the Schools Council and the Health Education Council with additional support from the Scottish Health Education Group and the Transport and Road Research Laboratory. However, the uptake of such resources appears to be limited, this most commonly being attributed by educationalists to their high cost and/or considerable time requirements. This is especially true when in-service training is a necessary pre-condition of using an alcohol education package with young people in schools.

The situation in Great Britain contrasts sharply with that in some other countries. For example, in the Scandinavian countries alcohol education is an integral part of the compulsory school curriculum. In addition, the school-based resources there are backed up by parallel campaigns in the community, thus reinforcing the educational message. In the United States the education system is, of course, much less centralised than it is in Britain and in some European countries. Nevertheless, many American schools include sophisticated alcohol education materials in their curriculum.

Bearing in mind the problems facing school-based alcohol education in Britain, is it possible to devise some kind of alcohol education programme which would be of practical value for teachers? What are the perceived needs of the 'consumers' of alcohol education resources? In other words, what kind of alcohol education programmes do educationalists themselves believe to be feasible in terms of implementation within the curriculum? In order to clarify such issues, the Alcohol Research Group at Edinburgh University conducted a pilot study in 1984. This exercise involved a postal survey of all local education authorities in the United Kingdom, and was aimed at directors of education and senior advisors. The results of this pilot study showed that senior educationalists were overwhelmingly in favour of some kind of alcohol education in secondary schools. However, it was also apparent that for any such education to be practically useful, it would have to be short, inexpensive (ideally free) and easy for teachers to use without in-service training or extensive preparation time. These constraints have been incorporated into the study described in this book.

THE PRESENT STUDY

The alcohol education initiative which forms the basis of this book is a primary prevention programme. It is a school-based intervention, targeted at all 12- to 13-year-old pupils and taught in the school by class teachers. An alcohol education package was developed which aimed to be acceptable to teachers in terms of the constraints identified above from the pilot study. The materials developed therefore had to be easy and attractive for teachers to use, demanding little in terms of preparation time or cost. The educational materials were designed to help young people begin to develop a responsible use of alcohol. The content emphasises issues which were identified as being particularly relevant to the target age group.

The principal aim of the study was to evaluate scientifically whether, in fact, such an alcohol education package could be effective.

The remainder of this book describes the study and its results. First, it sets the project in the broad context of health education (Chapter 1), with particular emphasis on evaluating the effectiveness of primary prevention programmes in curbing misuse of psychoactive substances among young people. In subsequent chapters, details will be given about how the study was conducted in schools, and the outcome of this evaluation research will be discussed. The implications of the findings will be considered not just in terms of school-based alcohol education, but in the broader context of health education for young people. Clearly, this book will be of particular interest to school-teachers, especially those involved in Personal and Social Education, Health Education or Guidance. However, the issues discussed concern all teachers, educational psychologists, health educators and parents, in fact, anyone who is involved with the well-being of young people in a professional capacity or otherwise. As a research monograph, the book should also be of interest to students of social science, especially those with an interest in survey methodology and educational research.

Chapter 1
Is alcohol education needed? How should it be done?

This chapter aims to assess the need for alcohol education against a background of information on levels of alcohol consumption. The main purpose of examining how alcohol is used in society will be to begin to answer the questions:

Is alcohol education necessary, especially for young people?
If so, what is the best way to go about it?

The first section will examine patterns of alcohol consumption in the general population, and will identify some of the factors which may influence individual drinking habits. The focus will then be placed on young people and drinking, and some possible explanations will be considered of why people use and/or misuse psychoactive substances. The role of these explanations will be examined in the context of theoretical models of health-related behaviour, emphasising the implications for primary prevention strategies. Finally, this chapter will review some of the evidence on the effectiveness of educating young people about alcohol and other drugs. Problems common to this kind of investigation will be acknowledged, and some consideration given as to how these might be tackled.

ALCOHOL CONSUMPTION IN THE UNITED KINGDOM – DO WE NEED TO BE EDUCATED?

In the United Kingdom, as in many other countries, alcohol is a legal drug, readily available and relatively inexpensive. It also plays an integral part in a wide range of social rituals, such as christenings, weddings and funerals. More generally, alcohol serves as a widely acceptable symbol of celebration, or simply as a social lubricant, oiling the wheels of social interaction. In view of this apparently widespread popularity, what can statistics tell us about the levels of alcohol consumption in the United Kingdom? How much do we drink? Do we drink more than we used to? And how do we compare to other countries?

Historical data suggest that consumption of alcohol in the United Kingdom has been at much higher levels in the past. For example, statistics from 1680 indicate an average beer consumption of 16.1 pints per person per week. The comparable figure for 1975 was roughly one quarter of this (Spring and Buss 1977).

More recent figures suggest that since 1960, total alcohol consumption in the United Kingdom has undergone a slow but steady increase. This is illustrated in Table 1.1.

The exception to this trend was in the period 1979–82 when there was a sharp drop in consumption. This corresponds to a temporary increase in the real price of alcohol during a general economic recession. Although consumption has been slowly increasing since 1982, the level for 1988 has still not reached the peak of 13.6 pints per head recorded in 1979. Overall, the total amount of alcohol drunk by the adult population in the United Kingdom has clearly increased considerably between 1970 and 1988. This increase, however, has not been consistent for all types of alcohol. As the right-hand columns in Table 1.1 illustrate, the increase in consumption has been much greater for wines and spirits than it has been for beer and cider.

How do these official statistics for alcohol consumption in the United Kingdom compare to those for other countries? Table 1.2 shows the alcohol consumption figures, per head of population, for forty-five 'leading' countries world-wide, ranging from 1970 to 1987.

Interpretation of these data indicates that in 1987 the United Kingdom ranked about half-way down the table in twenty-second position, with consumption levels consistently lower than many other countries in the world. Even if comparison is restricted only to European countries, the per capita consumption for the United Kingdom falls below that of many other countries. Within the European Community, only the Republic of Ireland drinks less than the United Kingdom. (This excludes Greece, because the statistics from that country do not include spirits, thus making comparison impossible.) During the period illustrated in Table 1.2, France held the 'top' position in the league with the highest recorded levels of alcohol consumption. However, it should also be noted that, unlike other European countries, the figures from France illustrate a steady downward trend.

Table 1.1 UK consumption of alcohol

Year	Alcohol consumption		Percentage share by type of drink based on alcohol content			
	Pints per head	Litres per head	Beer	Cider	Wine	Spirits
1960	7.6	4.3	73.5	1.6	7.7	17.2
1961	8.0	4.6	73.7	1.6	7.9	16.9
1962	8.0	4.5	73.3	1.4	8.1	17.2
1963	8.1	4.6	72.0	1.4	8.9	17.7
1964	8.6	4.9	71.3	1.4	9.3	18.1
1965	8.2	4.7	72.0	1.5	9.1	17.4
1966	8.5	4.9	72.3	1.6	9.2	17.0
1967	8.6	4.9	71.3	1.7	10.0	16.9
1968	8.8	5.0	70.3	1.7	10.8	17.1
1969	8.9	5.1	72.2	1.9	10.1	15.8
1970	9.3	5.3	70.4	2.0	10.4	17.2
1971	9.8	5.6	69.4	1.9	11.3	17.4
1972	10.3	5.9	67.3	1.8	12.1	18.8
1973	11.5	6.5	63.3	1.8	13.6	21.4
1974	12.0	6.8	61.9	1.7	13.7	22.7
1975	12.0	6.8	63.8	2.0	12.6	21.6
1976	12.3	7.0	62.4	2.3	11.9	23.5
1977	12.1	6.9	64.7	2.2	12.6	20.5
1978	13.1	7.5	61.5	2.0	13.6	22.9
1979	13.6	7.7	59.8	2.0	13.8	24.4
1980	12.8	7.3	59.1	2.1	14.5	24.3
1981	12.4	7.0	58.2	2.4	15.5	23.9
1982	12.2	6.9	58.3	2.9	15.9	22.9
1983	12.7	7.2	58.2	3.1	16.2	22.5
1984	12.6	7.2	56.6	3.1	17.9	22.5
1985	13.0	7.4	56.0	2.9	17.8	23.3
1986	12.9	7.4	55.7	3.0	18.1	23.2
1987	13.3	7.5	55.7	2.8	18.5	23.0
1988	13.4	7.6	55.5	2.7	18.1	23.7

Sources: HM Customs and Excise; Office of Population Censuses and Surveys.

In conclusion, official statistics such as those illustrated in Table 1.2 would suggest that less alcohol is drunk by adults in the United Kingdom than in many other countries either in Europe or worldwide. This could perhaps be interpreted as an indication that there is no real need to educate people in the United Kingdom about alcohol. However, the statistics reported in Table 1.1 indicate that, despite this apparently favourable comparison, there is no justification for complacency. Adults in the United Kingdom are drinking more

Table 1.2 Alcohol consumption per head in leading countries (litres per head of 100% alcohol)

	1970	1975	1980	1982	1983	1984	1985	1986	1987
Argentina	..	..	11.5	10.1	10.0	9.5	8.9	9.1	8.9
Australia	8.2	9.5	9.5	9.7	9.5	9.4	9.3	9.1	8.8
Austria	10.5	11.1	11.0	9.9	10.2	10.0	9.9	10.0	9.9
Belgium	9.0	10.0	10.8	10.7	10.6	10.7	10.4	10.1	10.7
Brazil (beer and wine)	0.7	1.0	1.3	1.5	1.4	1.4	1.4	1.9	1.9
Bulgaria	6.7	8.2	8.7	9.0	8.8	8.9	8.8	9.3	8.9
Cameroon	..	..	..	..	..	..	..	..	..
Canada	6.5	8.4	8.7	8.4	8.1	8.0	7.9	7.8	8.0
Chile (beer and wine)	5.8	5.4	6.5	6.2	5.4	5.5	5.6	5.6	5.2
China	..	..	..	..	..	..	..	..	..
Columbia (beer only)	1.7	1.6	2.2	2.3	2.6	2.5	2.8	2.6	..
Cuba	1.7	1.8	1.2	1.3	1.3	1.3	1.3	1.4	1.5
Czechoslovakia	8.4	9.2	9.6	9.8	9.6	9.5	9.4	9.0	8.6
Denmark	6.9	9.0	9.5	10.2	10.6	10.3	9.7	9.9	9.6
Finland	4.5	6.3	6.4	6.4	6.5	6.6	6.7	7.0	7.1
France	17.4	17.1	15.9	15.3	14.9	14.2	13.7	13.7	13.0
German DR	6.1	8.0	10.1	10.4	10.5	10.2	10.3	10.5	10.5
German FR	10.3	11.3	11.4	10.9	11.0	10.7	10.8	10.5	10.6
Greece (beer and wine)	5.3	5.3	6.7	6.8	6.8	6.8	6.8	6.2	5.4
Hungary	9.6	10.7	12.5	12.3	12.3	12.4	12.2	11.1	10.7
Ireland, Rep. of	5.8	7.3	7.4	6.7	6.1	6.2	6.6	6.6	5.4
Italy	14.2	13.2	12.3	12.4	11.7	11.5	11.0	10.0	10.0
Japan (includes saki)	4.9	5.4	5.7	5.8	6.2	6.2	6.1	6.2	6.3
Kenya	..	..	..	..	..	..	..	..	..
Korea, Rep. of	..	..	..	..	..	..	..	..	..
Mexico	2.2	2.4	2.9	2.9	2.7	2.6	2.8	3.5	1.8
Netherlands	5.6	8.8	8.8	8.6	8.9	8.6	8.5	8.6	8.3
New Zealand	6.4	7.9	8.1	8.3	7.8	8.2	7.9	8.3	8.3
Nigeria	..	..	..	..	..	..	..	..	..
Peru	2.4	3.5	4.6	4.5	4.5	4.4	4.6	4.9	2.2
Philippines	..	..	4.0	4.1	4.2	4.0	3.7	3.8	..
Poland	5.4	7.3	8.7	6.4	6.5	6.2	6.7	6.9	7.2
Portugal	9.8	13.1	10.0	11.8	13.4	12.4	12.9	11.2	10.5
Romania	6.1	7.6	7.9	7.6	7.7	7.7	7.7	5.4	7.6
South Africa	3.0	3.6	3.8	4.3	4.3	4.3	4.2	4.0	4.4
Spain	12.0	14.2	13.2	12.4	12.5	10.8	11.5	11.7	12.7
Sweden	5.8	6.4	6.4	5.6	5.3	5.3	5.3	5.7	5.4
Switzerland	10.3	10.2	10.6	11.1	10.9	10.9	10.9	10.7	11.0
Taiwan	..	..	..	..	..	..	..	..	..
Turkey	0.5	0.8	0.7	1.1	1.2	1.1	1.0	1.0	1.0
USA	6.9	7.7	8.2	8.1	8.0	7.8	7.7	7.6	7.6
USSR	6.5	6.0	6.2	6.0	6.1	6.7	5.7	3.5	3.2
Yugoslavia	7.9	8.1	7.8	8.2	8.1	8.1	7.7	8.1	7.6
Venezuela	2.5	2.5	3.8	3.7	3.6	3.6	3.1	3.1	3.7
Zaire (beer only)	0.0	1.0	0.5	0.5	0.5	0.5	0.5	0.5	..
UK	5.2	6.6	7.1	6.7	7.0	7.0	7.2	7.1	7.2

alcohol than they used to, albeit in a different kind of alcoholic beverage. Furthermore, there is confirmation in the Reports of the Royal College of Physicians (1987) and the Royal College of General Practitioners (1986) of the 'general view that alcohol related social, medical and economic problems have been rising over the post-war period' (Jackson 1989: 75).

The social costs of alcohol misuse have been estimated by health economists, but as they themselves have noted, the resulting figures, while clearly placing a burden on society, can only be regarded as an estimate. In addition to the more tangible costs of alcohol misuse such as occupancy of hospital beds and more general use of health service resources, there are many areas where accurate measurement is difficult, if not impossible. Alcohol, for example, is known to contribute to many accidents in the home and in the workplace, and to levels of absenteeism and reduced efficiency at work. Even more difficult to quantify is the cost of personal distress arising directly and indirectly from alcohol misuse. The direction in which estimates of these costs may err, however, is not universally accepted. McDonnell and Maynard (1985) have argued that the calculated costs can only be regarded as a 'conservative estimate'. On the other hand, it has been suggested that the economic costs of alcohol abuse calculated by the National Institute on Alcohol Abuse and Alcoholism in the USA are inaccurate and 'continually overstate actual costs'. The major explanation for this is seen to lie in the 'attribution of casuality to alcohol where none has been shown to exist, and improper methodology with regard to productivity impairment measures' (Heien and Pittman 1989: 567). Clearly this is an issue which will continue to be difficult to resolve.

As noted elsewhere (for example, Royal College of General Practitioners 1986; Anderson 1989) the precise relationship between public controls on the availability of alcohol, levels of consumption and the extent of alcohol-related problems is a complex and controversial issue.

A variety of strategies have been proposed to curb the extent of alcohol misuse and alcohol-related problems in the United Kingdom. Tether (1989) has classified the wide range of policy responses into three broad categories. One of these emphasises the links between rates of alcohol problems and levels of consumption. This perspective recommends that the availability of alcohol should be controlled by means of fiscal policies such as price regulations through taxation and liquor licensing restrictions. However, as already indicated, the effect of such controls on levels of consumption and alcohol-related problems is unclear (Duffy 1989). Levels of consumption in a general population form a spectrum ranging from very light drinkers at one extreme to very heavy drinkers at the other. The proportions of light, moderate and excessive drinkers will vary over time, and this has implications for overall levels of alcohol-related problems. Control policies at this level need to take account of the patterns of alcohol use within the general population. On the other hand, Kreitman (1986) has argued in favour of a health education strategy which has an overall aim of reducing alcohol consumption levels throughout the general population. Even if 'problem drinkers' were less likely than others to adopt the necessary changes (and this cannot be assumed), 'if the large, low-risk majority indeed halved their intake the gains would be so extensive as to more than offset the casualties continuing to be generated by the unreformed heavy consumers' (Kreitman 1986: 362).

An alternative category of response proposed by Tether focuses on problem drinkers, rather than on the product for consumption, and advocates policies which promote intervention amongst those perceived to be at risk from excessive consumption.

The third category of policy response as described by Tether focuses on:

> contemporary society, its *drinking patterns* and attitudes. The concern here is with such things as drinking for effect, to be tough, to solve problems, or to make difficult relationships or situations more bearable. Unhealthy drinking attitudes include the belief that all social occasions must be drinking occasions, that intoxication is something to be tolerated or even encouraged, or that drunkenness is an excuse for otherwise inexcusable behaviour. The preventive aim of those who focus on the way society uses alcohol, is to increase knowledge of its effects and to encourage moderate drinking and responsible hosting.
>
> (Tether 1989: 138)

Although these three approaches to curbing alcohol misuse are based on different assumptions, Tether emphasises the importance of an integrated response which incorporates strategies from the full range of possibilities.

It will become evident in subsequent chapters that the kind of educational responses to alcohol misuse discussed in this book can be most accurately classified in the last of these three categories. However, the limitations of seeking to curb alcohol misuse by employing only one approach will frequently be acknowledged with a plea for reinforcement by alternative strategies.

The discussion above concerning levels of alcohol consumption amongst the general population has highlighted a fundamental requirement in all efforts to curb alcohol misuse. This is the need for information on patterns of alcohol use within a population, and some explanation of why people use and/or misuse alcohol in the way that they do. The remainder of this section will address these issues as a preliminary to establishing a model of alcohol use amongst young people.

WHY DO PEOPLE MISUSE ALCOHOL AND OTHER DRUGS?

In order to prevent the misuse of alcohol and other psychoactive substances, it is necessary to have some ideas about *why* they are used, and in what way. This is a complex task. Many people are familiar with the popular stereotypes of 'the drug addict' (usually a young scruffy person, probably male) and the 'alcoholic' (typically a derelict, homeless male). Another recent innovation is the so-called 'lager lout', portrayed as young, noisy, unkempt, drunken and trouble seeking. Such stereotypes have great 'comfort value' (Cohen 1972) in that they isolate socially 'deviant' behaviours by creating exaggerated and remote scapegoats, who can subsequently take the blame for all kinds of social problems. The characteristics of such stereotypes, however, are open to question. For example, in a report summarising the United Kingdom government's strategy for tackling use of illicit drugs, it was noted that:

> There is no single cause of drug misuse. It is not even possible to say with any confidence what the main factors are. Many explanations have been offered: ready availability of drugs, personality defects, poor home background, peer group pressure, poor relationships, lack of self-esteem, youthful experimentation and rebellion, boredom and unemployment. All of these factors probably play some part. But there is no convincing evidence that any one – or any combination – of these factors is of greater significance than the rest.
>
> (Home Office 1985: paragraph 1.8)

An earlier report on treatment and rehabilitation by the Advisory Council on the Misuse of Drugs had noted a similar difficulty in classifying drug misusers:

> The majority [of drug misusers] are relatively stable individuals who have more in common with the general population than with any essentially pathological sub-groups. . . . There is no evidence of any uniform personality characteristic or type of person who becomes either an addict or an individual with drug problems.
>
> (Department of Health and Social Security 1982: paragraph 5.3)

The complex aetiology of alcohol and other drug use has been the focus of a considerable amount of research. This has identified a confusing and contradictory array of factors which influences both the use and misuse of psychoactive substances such as alcohol, tobacco, prescribed and illegal drugs (Fazey 1977; Plant 1981; Peck 1982). These influences have been shown to operate at all levels, from social policy to individual characteristics. But as noted in a recent report on prevention strategies, again by the Advisory Council on the Misuse of Drugs 'while there has been a considerable amount of research into why people misuse drugs, no single cause, or consistent pattern of multiple causes, has been identified' (Home Office 1984: paragraph 2.2).

The next section will consider some of these influences in the context of alcohol consumption.

The role of economic factors in alcohol consumption has already been briefly acknowledged. There is some evidence from the United Kingdom that as the real price of alcohol (to the consumer) decreases there is an increase in consumption and alcohol-related problems (Royal College of Psychiatrists 1986; Sales *et al.* 1989). However, as noted above, the overall effect of alcohol control policy on levels of consumption and harm is unclear.

Other economic factors such as personal income and employment status have been associated with the pattern of alcohol use and misuse amongst adults. A number of population surveys have demonstrated that respondents who were unemployed were more likely to be heavy drinkers (Crawford *et al.* 1987). It is not clear, however, whether or not unemployment leads to heavy drinking, or vice versa (Winton *et al.* 1986).

A variety of social factors have been shown to have an important influence on the way individuals use and misuse alcohol. Amongst these, one of the most controversial issues is the influence of alcohol advertising. This debate is pursued in Grant and Ritson (1983). Following a review of some of the available research on this complex issue, these authors concluded:

The debate therefore remains inconclusive. Advertising of alcoholic drinks may have some effect on overall consumption but does certainly have a significant effect on brand choice. It may also be important in subtly distilling and reinforcing the fantasy images of virility or sophistication which surround alcohol. . . . A ban on advertising might be taken as a mark of the community's seriousness of intent as far as alcohol misuse is concerned, but this would be at a cost to individual freedom. . . . For the time being, national restriction rather than total prohibition seems the most appropriate and the most acceptable approach.

(Grant and Ritson 1983: 117)

In the context of young people, more recent research suggests that, despite the restrictions which operate on alcohol advertising, these advertisements still capture the attention of young people. A study of 10- to 16-year-olds in Glasgow schools examined which aspects of advertisements (not just those for alcoholic products) held particular appeal for this age group. These were found to include humour, colour and music, which it is argued are often found in alcohol advertisements. More specifically the authors concluded that for this age group their findings 'suggest that advertisements for alcoholic drinks become increasingly salient and attractive' (Aitken *et al.* 1988: 1).

However, images of alcohol are not restricted to product advertisements. The portrayal of alcohol in the mass media, especially in television drama, is not subject to restrictive advertising codes, and it has to be noted that at the time of writing, one of the most popular 'soap-operas' on British television is set in a London pub. Hansen (1986) examined the media portrayal of alcohol in a variety of contexts (fiction, news/documentary and advertisements) on the four television channels in the United Kingdom for a period of two weeks. He concluded that overall the drinking of alcohol was presented as natural; there was very little portrayal of negative consequences and the issue of alcohol consumption was seldom discussed. He concluded that such examples were not conducive to learning about the real-life role of alcohol. The influence of such role-modelling is, of course, virtually impossible to assess.

Although all members of society are subject to social influences on their alcohol consumption, this is an especially important aspect of young people's use of alcohol and other drugs. One study which examined these influences in depth was conducted by O'Connor

(1978). This survey comprised approximately 2,000 interviews on a sample of Irish, Anglo-Irish and English 18- to 21-year-olds, their mothers and their fathers. The sample was chosen to enable the author to investigate the contribution of parental, peer-group, ethnic/cultural and social/personal influences on youthful alcohol consumption. O'Connor found that the most important aspect of parental influence was the attitudes of the parents towards drinking, most especially those of the father. This was found to have a greater influence on children's levels of consumption than either parental drinking behaviour or general family relationships. Similar findings have been reported in several American surveys (Akers 1968; Bacon and Jones 1968; Fontane and Layne 1979; Rachal *et al.* 1975). In the light of such evidence, Gordon and McAlister concluded that:

> The abstaining adolescent is most likely to come from abstaining parents, the moderate drinker from moderately drinking parents and heavy drinkers, in disproportionate numbers, either from homes where one or both parents are heavy drinkers or from homes where both are abstainers.
>
> (Gordon and McAlister 1982: 206)

The latter finding also emerged from a survey of 10- to 14-year-olds in Scotland, which indicated that children whose parents were total abstainers from alcohol were more likely to indulge in under-age consumption of alcohol (Davies and Stacey 1972).

In O'Connor's study of Irish, Anglo-Irish and English families, ethnic origin on its own did not explain youthful drinking behaviour. However, it was found to have a strong influence on the aspects of parental attitudes, which in turn had a strong influence on offspring's alcohol consumption, as noted above.

Peer group pressure is a further social influence acknowledged to play an important role in the way young people use and/or misuse alcohol. As with other studies of alcohol and other drugs, O'Connor (1978) found that as the child grows older, friends provide the overall context and location for drinking. Support from friends for drinking was found to be the most powerful peer group influence, and this was higher for males.

In addition to the social pressures discussed above, the role of individual factors such as developmental maturity, heredity and personality have been acknowledged (Gordon and McAlister 1982). In the specific context of young people, gender also appears to be an important influence on the use of alcohol. There is considerable evidence from surveys that adolescent males are more likely than their female counterparts to have had their first experience of alcohol at an earlier age. Throughout adolescence males are also more likely to drink alcohol more often than females. This is true not just for youngsters in the United Kingdom (Plant *et al.* 1985; Marsh *et al.* 1986; Bagnall 1988) but also in Finland (Ahlström 1987) and the United States of America (Johnston *et al.* 1977). Once again there is an indication that cultural and peer group influences play an important role in relation to youthful drinking habits. But how much misuse of alcohol is involved in these habits? This question can be broadly answered with reference to official statistics concerning alcohol-related offences. Although not restricted to under-age drinking, the examples below serve to reinforce the extent to which some of the problems associated with intoxication are most likely to be experienced by young people in Britain. In this context a major cause of concern is that of road traffic accidents and vehicle offences. Official statistics in 1985 for England and Wales indicated that the proportion of drivers and (motor-cycle) riders involved in an accident and who subsequently failed a breath test peaked at age 20 to 24 (Home Office Standing Conference 1987). Furthermore, in a report aptly titled *The Quiet Massacre*, Dunbar (1985) noted that of the 1,200 annual fatalities resulting from drinking and driving, 600 were young people in their teens or twenties. Clearly the combination of inexperience in driving skills and alcohol misuse can all too often be a recipe for disaster.

Public concern about alcohol misuse amongst young people motivated the United Kingdom government in 1986 to set up a special committee to examine this issue. The resulting report, *Young People and Alcohol*, noted that 'under-age drinking is only a part of the wider problem of alcohol misuse in society, and consideration of it cannot be entirely isolated from the other issues' (Home Office Standing Conference 1987: 19). This report, however, also identified some of the main features which distinguish youthful alcohol misuse:

(i) under-age drinking PER SE has legal consequences for the drinker and supplier;
(ii) under-age drinking involves a particularly vulnerable section of the population;
(iii) whereas for adults society generally takes the view that they should be allowed relatively unrestricted access to alcohol, it is

accepted that there should be strict restrictions upon the drinking of the young;
(iv) the young are especially susceptible to the effects of alcohol.
(Home Office Standing Conference 1987: 19)

In line with these characteristics, this report included recommendations for changes in alcohol taxation, stricter enforcement of the laws to curb under-age drinking and severe restrictions on alcohol advertising and sponsorship. Furthermore, a strong plea is made for educating young people about responsible use of alcohol.

From the discussion in this section, it is clear that substance use and misuse cannot be viewed in isolation. They occur as all social behaviours occur, within a framework of cultural, political and individual factors. The resultant effect of any drug is a product of the drug, the user and the environment.

SOME THEORETICAL EXPLANATIONS

Theories of substance use and their implications for prevention are of little value unless they take account of the wide range of potential influences on substance use identified above. The complexity of the forces at work is illustrated in depth by the 'problem behaviour theory' of Jessor and Jessor (1977). Their theory 'rests upon the social-psychological relationships that obtain within and between each of three major systems – the personality system, the perceived environment system and the behavior system' (Jessor and Jessor 1977: 19). The basis of this theory has already been touched on above in a simplistic sense, in that substance use behaviour is seen to be influenced by personal factors such as attitudes, beliefs and 'cognitions' in addition to social learning through modelling and reinforcement. The Jessors have argued that:

> The dynamics of the behavior system depend on the meanings or significance – the functions – attached to the actions involved. It is this fact, that social psychologically defined behavior has such meanings or significance, that connects behavior with its conceptual determinants in the personality and the perceived environment.
> (Jessor and Jessor 1977: 37)

The Jessors have suggested that heavy drinking is associated with a variety of factors, all of which are themselves associated with tolerance of deviance and risk-taking behaviours. This 'problem behaviour theory' is characteristic of social psychological theories which are based on the assumption that most social behaviours, including those relating to health and substance use, are largely a result of rational decision-making processes (for example, Fishbein 1980; Ajzen and Fishbein 1980, Triandis 1980). Conscious decisions about whether or not to engage in a specific behaviour (such as, for example, having a drink of alcohol) are termed behaviour intentions. These are seen to mediate between the attitudes that individuals hold and their actual behaviour (see Fishbein 1980). The more positive the attitude, the more positive the behavioural intention will be, and the greater the likelihood of that behaviour being carried out. Grube and Morgan have reported high levels of consistency (using data from survey questionnaires) between self-reported measures of behavioural intentions and substance use (Grube and Morgan 1986). However, as also noted in their report 'If the individual does not possess the skills or knowledge required to achieve a behavioural outcome, or if the opportunity to engage in the behaviour does not arise, the intentions may not predict performance' (Grube and Morgan 1986: 5).

What are the implications of such theoretical explanations of substance use behaviour? In particular, how can they help us to develop appropriate measures to prevent drug-related harm? One way to answer this is to simplify the ideas into a model which can help us to understand and explain health-related behaviour. In a social scientific sense, a model is a simplification which is used to extract the most important features of a system and to highlight the interrelationships between these features. It follows that a model which explains health-related behaviour, albeit in a simplified form, can assist in the process of developing approaches to health education. One such model is the 'epidemiological triangle' proposed by De Haes (1987). This model provides a 'balanced view' of some of the main factors postulated to determine psychoactive substance use. This is illustrated in Figure 1.1.

Although outwardly simple, De Haes's model clearly identifies the permanent interconnections between the three principal influences – the individual, the substance and the context. As a tool to assist the development of drug education, this model or explanation of drug-related behaviour clearly suggests that educational programmes based on individual factors in isolation are unlikely to be effective because they do not take account of either the specific drug or of the context of its use. The same prediction of ineffectiveness would hold

14   Educating young drinkers

```
                Individual
                   /\
                  /  \
                 /    \
                /      \
               /        \
              /          \
             /            \
            /              \
           /_____\
     Substance              Context
```

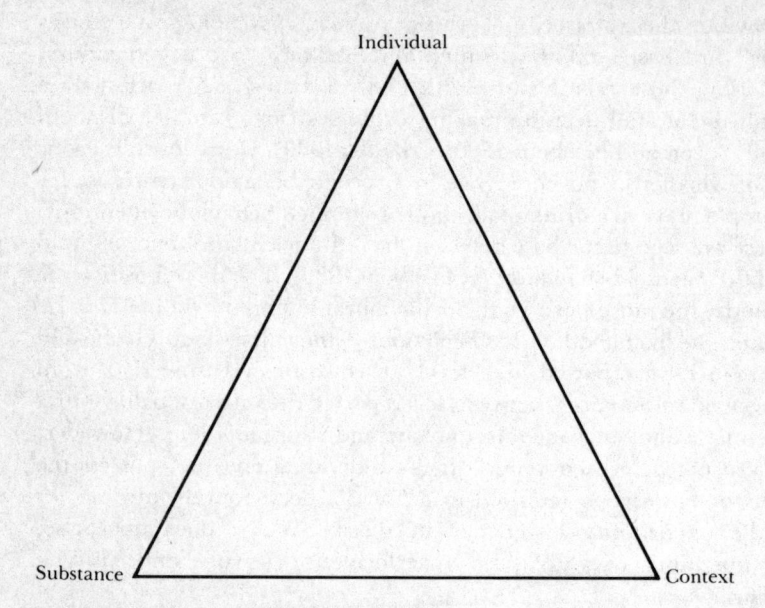

Figure 1.1 The epidemiological triangle

for a programme which is merely drug based. Such predictions have indeed been supported and the evidence will be elaborated below.

A more complex model is the 'Health Action Model' proposed by Tones (1987a). Although this was developed in a context of health-related behaviour in general, it is readily applied to the more specific context of drug use and misuse. Tones's model emphasises the potential 'barriers' to healthy behaviour and their relationship with each other. These barriers are identified at various levels ranging from individual ignorance to cultural belief systems and government policies. As already noted above, such influences have been well documented in surveys of psychoactive drug use and may be particularly relevant to the health-related behaviour of adolescents.

Theoretical models such as the two described above help to clarify the major issues which have to be addressed in developing any preventive measures in health education. In addition, they make it possible to target preventive programmes at specific aspects of health-related behaviour, and to highlight the limitations of any one particular initiative. These issues are crucial in any attempt to measure and compare the effectiveness of different interventions.

ALCOHOL EDUCATION AND ITS EVALUATION – SOME KEY ISSUES

The preceding sections have perhaps painted a somewhat gloomy picture of the complexity of health-related behaviour and therefore of developing effective preventive or harm minimisation measures. Certainly this difficulty is not eased by narrowing the context from health education in general to alcohol and other drugs. Here too, it would seem unlikely that programmes could be devised to counteract the range of factors which influence such behaviour. The complexity of the problem in relation to alcohol consumption amongst young people has been noted by Grant:

> In societies like Britain, Ireland, the United States and other northern industrialised nations . . . despite the ambivalence of the value systems, despite the pluralistic nature of the social networks, learning to drink is one important demonstration of the ritual passage from childhood into adulthood. Although occasionally this passage is associated with rebellion, with experimentation and with repeated excessive consumption, far more frequently it is sanctioned, even encouraged, by the adult population.
> (Grant 1982: 13)

Hamburg (1989) has also acknowledged the appeal of alcohol (and tobacco) to adolescents as a symbol of adulthood, and attributes this to the fact that use of these substances is socially and legally acceptable for adults but widely prohibited for adolescents. He reiterates the ambivalent nature of social attitudes referred to above by Grant:

> At a time when many illegal drugs are readily available – marijuana and hashish, LSD, amphetamines, tranquillisers, cocaine and heroin – adults are often more comfortable when adolescents choose to use the legal substances with which the older generations are familiar. Therefore, some adults encourage adolescents in the use of alcohol and tobacco in the hope of deterring them from using illegal drugs that are perceived as more threatening.
> (Hamburg 1989: 139)

Even if alcohol education ventures are initiated, is it possible to measure their effect on individual behaviour? These issues are fundamental to the study which forms the heart of this book and therefore merit some further discussion.

Developing alcohol education – some underlying assumptions

Alcohol education, as all health education, must in its broadest sense be viewed as a political issue. Few health educators would disagree that a basic prerequisite of any health education programme is a set of clear objectives, and of well-defined procedures designed to achieve them. This statement, however, already serves to indicate the political implications of any health education initiative. For example, who decides what the objectives should be; what criteria determine the procedures selected to achieve them? Clearly there is no definitive answer to such questions, any response being bound at least by ideological perspectives and/or by whatever model of health education is adopted. In Britain, a considerable body of criticism has arisen which questions some of the traditional values and assumptions underlying the conventional approach to much health education. In particular, doubt has been raised about the validity of emphasising individual choice and responsibility in health-related behaviour, at the expense of socio-economic factors beyond the control of the individual. Such doubt has been clearly articulated in a case study by Farrant and Russell (1986) who use prevention of coronary heart disease as an illustration of the politics which underlie the production of publications in health promotion campaigns. It is also neatly summed up in a collection of edited chapters on the politics of health education, where it is argued by one of the contributors that: 'Three major criticisms can be levelled against individualistic health education: first, it denies that health is a social product; second it assumes free choice exists; third it is not effective within its own terms of reference' (Naidoo 1986: 19).

The 'individualistic' approach identified above is sometimes referred to as 'victim blaming' and has been equated with the individualism of right-wing politics. This argument can be illustrated by taking the example of a mother of young children who lives soley on state benefits in damp and deprived accommodation. The major concern for such a single-parent family is likely to be to improve the basic living conditions, and so basic health status. Healthy life-style issues, such as low-fat diet or reduced alcohol consumption may be of little interest to individuals living in circumstances of this kind. In addition, of course, it has been argued that the alternative diet proposed by health campaigners is more expensive than its less healthy equivalent. Individual choice in such issues is therefore externally constrained with political and social status creating barriers to the uptake of 'healthy behaviours'. The content of health promotion campaigns is traditionally handed down 'from above', largely by medical experts. As noted by Farrant and Russell:

> the prescriptive style of health education communication, . . . can be seen as reinforcing the traditional 'active-and-dominant expert, passive-and-dependent-client' model of interaction that has been identified as a barrier to people acting individually and collectively to take control of their own health.
>
> (Farrant and Russell 1986: 14)

These authors go on to argue that 'the limitations imposed on health education by adopting an individualistic "top-down" approach result in educational initiatives which have little relevance to the actual health-related experience and consequent needs of the target audience'.

It may be necessary, at this point, to make a distinction between what is meant by health education and health promotion. These two terms are often used interchangeably, and their meanings undeniably overlap. There are, however, subtle differences which have important implications for any discussion of school-based alcohol education. Health *education* has been defined as 'any combination of learning opportunities designed to facilitate voluntary adaptation of behaviour which will improve or maintain health' (Green 1979: 162). Health *promotion* is a more broadly based concept which includes the organisational and political interventions required to ease such changes in health-related behaviour. Criticisms of health education such as these referred to above can more accurately be attributed to health promotion.

School-based alcohol education, therefore, as the focus of this book, is an example of health education, where exposure to specific learning opportunities is intended to help individuals to change (or to adopt) healthy behaviours in relation to alcohol use. Health promotion in the context of alcohol would have to go beyond this to include some of the interventions in the economic and political spheres identified in the preceding sections.

Nevertheless, even within the terms of the above definition, health education which places emphasis on individual control over health-related behaviours can still be regarded as controversial. Tones (1987b) has argued that in order to achieve a goal of voluntarism and genuine informed choice, social awareness of health risks must be combined with 'self empowerment'. This could be taken to indicate that there is little point in making people more aware of the health risks in their own lives unless they also acquire the means to reduce these risks. Tones has explained the concept of self-empowerment by dividing it into three main components – self-esteem, locus of control and social skills. Self-esteem can be equated with 'having the courage of your convictions'. Thus individuals with high self-esteem are more likely to behave in a way which is consistent with their beliefs. They should also be less likely to succumb to social pressures which conflict with personal beliefs. Perceived locus of control is associated with the individual belief that personal action is possible, in order to reach a desired goal. Finally, appropriate social skills have to be selected and executed to achieve the intended result.

The balance between these three components of 'self-empowerment' will determine the actual behaviour executed. Even if the desire to behave in a specific way is present along with a belief in the ability to do so, absence of the necessary social skills (for example, the assertiveness skills required to resist peer group pressure) will prevent the desired behaviour from being achieved. Change in any one of these components will therefore be a necessary but not in itself sufficient outcome of any health educational intervention aiming to bring about behaviour change.

This interrelationship between beliefs, social skills and behaviour is commonly synthesised in the term 'life skills', particularly in the context of health or personal and social education. Tones (1987b), however, has cautioned against indiscriminate use of this popular terminology which he has argued could be interpreted as a means of social control. Rather, the development of life skills should emphasise personal growth and an increasing awareness of self-determination. This in turn can lead to collective action through pressure group activity, community action or political party membership.

In the context of alcohol education in schools, this book proposes that it is possible to produce materials which can be viewed within this kind of perspective, that is, one which presents health education as a potential vehicle for social as well as for individual change. An alcohol education package of this kind would aim to increase individual awareness, not simply of the effects of alcohol, but also of the kinds of social pressures influencing its consumption, and of the skills required to deal with these pressures. Such an approach could arguably be the first step towards ultimate social change through collective social action. This argument is reflected in the World Health Organization's statement that 'education . . . has to do with the creation of social awareness. If the political will of the people is to be stimulated then education must play a central part in that process' (World Health Organization 1982).

Perhaps such change is under way in the context of tobacco smoking. As will become evident in the next section, one of the few applications of drug education to have provided some evidence of effectiveness is tobacco education for young people. Furthermore, although progress often takes time, there is little doubt that cigarette smoking in many countries is much less socially acceptable than it was twenty years ago. In many workplaces and public areas in the United Kingdom, 'No Smoking' is increasingly the norm, with provision reluctantly being provided for smokers. It can be argued that such social changes have arisen through pressure group activity, itself escalating through increased public awareness of the health risks of tobacco consumption. Furthermore, these changes are reflected in national statistics, where there is clear evidence that fewer people smoke tobacco regularly (Goddard and Ikin 1987). This issue will be considered again in the section devoted specifically to tobacco education programmes.

As noted in the Introduction, alcohol education in some form is not a new idea and has been available at least since the days of the Old Testament. Even then, people were aware of some of the risks of alcohol misuse although, as also noted in the Introduction, some of the advice was conflicting. It would appear that simply warning people of these risks really has little effect on consumption. The key point is, therefore, not just to provide information and warnings about alcohol, but to establish a form of alcohol education which can be shown to be effective.

Much literature is available which reports on effective health promotion/education campaigns. Some of these claim to have been effective simply on the basis that a large proportion of the general public said they are aware of specific campaigns. However, there is no evidence to suggest that such increased awareness on its own is sufficient to bring about change in health-related behaviour. More information is required about which particular aspects of a health education programme will most likely lead to behavioural change. Furthermore, such information must be based on carefully designed research, otherwise it is of little practical value. But is it possible to collect such information, especially in the context of education about substance misuse? The remainder of this chapter will provide a review of some studies which have attempted to do this. These will be restricted to some school- and college-based programmes relating to alcohol, drug and tobacco education for young people. Before reviewing these studies, a brief note must be made of the scientific basis of this kind of research.

Evaluation methodology

Two basic requirements underlie studies designed to evaluate the effectiveness of health education: (a) pre- and post-intervention measures, (b) a control group.

(a) Pre- and post-intervention measures

When looking at the effect of any intervention or treatment, it is necessary to have some information about the situation before the intervention. This is the pre-intervention (or baseline) measure. The effect of the intervention or treatment can then be assessed by examining the same information after the intervention. This is the post-intervention measure.

(b) Control group

Any study examining the effects of an intervention such as alcohol education requires two groups of people. The only difference between these two groups should be that one, the intervention group, receive the treatment or intervention and the second, the control group, does not. When the two groups are compared after the treatment or intervention any differences between them can be attributed to the intervention.

Without using pre- and post-intervention measures and a control group, it is not scientifically valid to conclude that a particular intervention has resulted in a particular change of behaviour. Nevertheless, this has not prevented such claims being made, not least in studies concerned with evaluating the effectiveness of educating young people about drugs misuse.

Has preventive education been effective?

Generally, the literature on the effectiveness of substance misuse education paints a pessimistic picture, suggesting that the majority of programmes are ineffective if not counterproductive (Kinder, *et al.* 1980; Schaps, *et al.* 1981; Bagnall and Plant 1987; De Haes 1987).

In a paper reviewing adolescent health care and prevention of disease in the Americas, Hamburg concluded:

> Research is greatly needed with regard to developmentally appropriate and culturally relevant educational efforts regarding substance abuse. In the United States much of the drug education has been ineffective or counterproductive. There is still a great deal to be learned about linking adolescent cognitive level, motivational structures and active learning techniques with informational content in ways that can catch and hold adolescents' attention and teach them what they need to know to avoid harmful practices and promote health.
>
> (Hamburg 1989: 145)

The task of reviewing the effectiveness of different approaches to substance misuse education is further compounded by the fact that some programmes address only one substance, while others address alcohol, tobacco and illicit drugs. However, as noted above, the one context in which effectiveness of substance misuse education has been well documented is that of tobacco smoking. In addition, this also appears to be the context which has produced the most evidence of effective interventions.

Tobacco education, at least in North America, would appear to be the first of the substance misuse education contexts to shift away from the conventional fear-arousal approaches, which were seldom shown to have any positive impact, to interventions which took account of psychosocial factors on smoking, especially amongst young people. Most of the recent programmes based on this model of health-related behaviour help students to become aware of the social pressures on them to smoke tobacco, and to develop techniques for resisting these pressures. The two principal methods have included videofilm as a stimulus to class discussion (for example, Evans *et al.* 1978) or peer-led discussion and role-playing (McAlister *et al.* 1979; McAlister *et al.* 1980). This type of intervention strategy is generally reported to have reduced new cigarette smoking by at least 50 per cent. Similar results were found when an alternative psychosocial strategy was adopted (Botvin 1982). This alternative approach focused on the development of life skills, with the intention of improving general personal competence. This clearly has close links with the concept of self-esteem discussed above.

It was noted above that national surveys in the United Kingdom suggested, in the early 1980s, a decline in the prevalence of smoking among young people. It was also evident, however, that the decline was accounted for by adults giving up smoking, rather than by young people failing to start (Marsh 1984; Dobbs and Marsh 1984). This was disappointing for health educationalists who had hoped that the decline indicated effective tobacco education. Nevertheless, some tobacco education initiatives around this time were shown to be effective, although many, as noted by Gillies (1986), were not evaluated, or if they were they failed to use a controlled study, pre- or post-intervention measures, or long-term follow-up. Gillies reported on six tobacco education studies in Britain which did include a controlled evaluation method using pre- and post-intervention measures, although only a short-term follow-up was incorporated. Of these six studies, three demonstrated that the tobacco education had produced a small effect on the tobacco-related knowledge of the young target group. Only one of these studies, however, succeeded in producing evidence for behaviour change as a result of the intervention (Ledwith and Osman 1985). This study differed from the others reviewed in that it had emphasised active learning, and included practical illustrations of the physiological effects of tobacco, and discussion about the influence of tobacco advertising. In her own controlled evaluation study, Gillies adopted a similar approach to tobacco education, with the two-fold aim of imparting knowledge about the effects of tobacco, and developing some understanding of the various social pressures to smoke. An additional important aspect of the programme which formed the basis of her evaluation was the close involvement of parents. Active parental participation in tobacco education projects in Norway had already been shown to increase the likelihood of preventing youthful uptake of smoking (Aaro *et al.* 1983). Taught as part of a school science project, the tobacco education intervention in Gillies's evaluation study was successful, in that for some of the participating schools the reduction in the uptake of smoking was greater amongst pupils exposed to the intervention than amongst controls. However, because of its multifaceted approach, this education evaluation was not able to draw precise conclusions about why there was an impact only in some schools, or what particular aspects of the programme had contributed to its effectiveness.

In comparison to tobacco education, the search for effective interventions on the use of illicit drugs has been less fruitful. During the early 1980s an experimental study of cannabis education was conducted on 4,000 students at schools in the Province of Ontario, Canada (Smart 1989). The resources made available to schools included videos, written materials and booklets with information about cannabis for young people. These were distributed to students, teachers and parents. The aim of this study was to measure the effect of increased exposure to cannabis education on subsequent levels of use. It did not attempt to clarify the effectiveness of one specific approach to such education. The results suggested that increased exposure to cannabis education was not associated with reduced use of that substance. This reinforces the argument that the important consideration in substance use education is the nature of the educational approach adopted.

An excellent recent review of drug education has been produced by De Haes (1987). It will be recalled that this author proposed the model of substance use behaviour illustrated in 'the epidemiological triangle' of Figure 1.1. This model evolved from an evaluation study of drug education programmes for 14- to 16-year-olds in Rotterdam (De Haes and Schuurman 1975). The study compared three approaches to drug education − a warning approach, an information approach and a person-oriented approach. The results of this study led the authors to conclude that substance-based programmes of the first two types should not be encouraged, as they could increase the risk of experimentation with drugs. The third approach, however, was effective in reducing drug experimentation.

From his comprehensive review of drug education, De Haes concluded that:

> It has become more and more clear that providing information about substances is not the most important element of effective 'drug education'. If one wants to work on prevention of drug use, it is first necessary to pay attention to young people and their problems. The promotion of 'balanced thinking' about drugs and drug users is needed, in order to create an atmosphere in which 'drug use' is just one of the 'facts of life' that young people are confronted by and must deal with.
>
> (De Haes 1987: 433)

Sadly, reviews of educational interventions focusing on alcohol have resulted in conclusions which are similarly negative to those for illicit drug use. For example, Grant concluded from a review of the evaluation of alcohol education in Western Europe and North America that 'past alcohol education has been a spectacularly wasteful enterprise'. Furthermore, he claimed that 'most programmes are directed towards illusory targets and pursue elusive goals' (Grant

1986: 198). Some of the difficulties of educating young people about alcohol are highlighted in a recent experimental evaluation in Canada of two linked alcohol education programmes for pupils aged 13 to 14 years respectively (Smart 1989). This study complemented the cannabis education study in Ontario noted above. The resources included lesson plans with activities for pupils and information sheets for teachers. Extensive in-service training was provided in advance of the alcohol programme, supplemented with on-going support for staff during the teaching. The implementation of this programme was associated with a decrease in the proportion of drinkers, especially among the younger students. It is important to note, however, that the alcohol education appeared to have little impact on heavy drinkers. Unfortunately this was not a controlled study, and therefore it is impossible to estimate how much the programme itself had contributed to these changes in drinking behaviour.

As Gordon and McAlister (1982) have noted, past alcohol education, especially in North America, has tended to place emphasis on the immorality of alcohol consumption, or on fear tactics. More recently the emphasis has shifted, especially in programmes targeted at adolescents, to focus on the physiological and social consequences of prolonged and heavy alcohol consumption. Such programmes, however, are acknowledged to have had little impact on older adolescents, and in some cases, as with illicit drugs education, it has been suggested that the intervention increased the likelihood of experimentation with alcohol (Stuart 1974). One frequently cited explanation for this failure is the argument that a predominantly negative and one-sided approach to alcohol education reduces the credibility of the content to the recipients. Thus although many people drink alcohol, only a small percentage of the general population will experience the problems of heavy and prolonged misuse. Emphasis on this aspect of consumption is therefore outside the personal experience of many adolescents, and certainly has little relevance to their everyday life-styles.

This issue of relevance and credibility to the target audience has also been raised by Finn (1977), who has criticised the majority of alcohol education resources for failing to acknowledge the significant ways in which alcohol gives pleasure. He has recommended that at least 25 per cent of any alcohol education programme ought to be concerned with the positive aspects of alcohol consumption. At the same time, Finn has acknowledged the need to avoid 'stigmatising' abstainers. This he argued can be done in two ways – first, by avoiding in educational materials any reference, explicit or implied, to UNIVERSAL pleasures of alcohol, and second, by including in 'decision-making' activities discussion about reasons for *not* drinking. The positive aspects of alcohol, and its legal consumption without seriously harmful consequences by many people perhaps indicate a need for alcohol to be given separate consideration in a generalised drug education programme.

In a review of seventy-eight alcohol education programmes, Grant (1982) noted a general trend which appeared common to all programmes. It appeared that more passive modes of communication were likely to have any impact only on alcohol-related knowledge. He also reported that single-lesson programmes were usually ineffective.

In recommending sustained interventions, Grant noted that 'most youth-targeted alcohol education programmes take little account of either parents or peers'. This led him to argue that:

> It comes as no surprise to young people to learn that drunk people crash their cars or that alcoholics die of liver cirrhosis. More to the point, perhaps, would be an educational approach which dealt with the influences (parents, peers, the media) upon young people's drinking, rather than one which, taking these influences for granted, concentrated upon what may well be perceived as depersonalised effects.
>
> (Grant 1982: 14)

Studies such as those referred to above obviously raise questions about the value of pursuing alcohol and drug education initiatives, especially amongst 'normal' adolescent and student populations. However, this negative view may not be justified and pessimism should be guarded. It has already become evident that many so-called 'evaluation' studies have not conformed to the quasi-experimental design outlined on page 36. Furthermore, as Milgram (1987) has noted, critics of drug and alcohol education programmes frequently fail to take account of different evaluation strategies and, perhaps more importantly, of different educational approaches. For example, some evaluations have concluded that educational intervention actually *increased* subsequent experimentation with illicit drugs (Swisher *et al.* 1971; Stuart 1974; Kinder *et al.* 1980; De Haes 1987). It is of crucial importance to note, however, that such findings have all concerned programmes which focused on substance-based information and warnings of dangers. It may therefore have been this specific approach which was counterproductive and not simply drugs education *per se*. It is interesting and somewhat depressing to reflect that scare tactics underlay the approach adopted by the government mass media campaigns in England and Wales during 1985 and 1986 to combat heroin use (see Plant 1987).

An alternative educational approach in some recent studies has produced more favourable results. This approach emphasises the personal and social skills involved in substance use and misuse. As noted earlier, such skills are required to handle influences on the use of alcohol and other drugs such as peer group pressure or parental expectations. This skills-based approach appears to have been particularly effective in the context of tobacco education. Success was reported in a tobacco education programme for 9- to 11-year-olds in England (Gillies and Wilcox 1984) using such educational methods. Furthermore, the follow-up results in the North Karelia Youth Project in Finland (Vartiainen, *et al.* 1986) would suggest that this kind of strategy may have a lasting effect on tobacco consumption, with measured differences between intervention and control groups in this study remaining after four years.

This alternative 'social skills' approach clearly shifts the emphasis away from the psychoactive substance in isolation. As we have seen, this is the kind of approach implied by Tones's health action model and De Haes's epidemiological triangle model, as described in the first section.

It has proved difficult to find evidence from studies which have evaluated a 'social skills' approach in the specific context of alcohol education for young people. Such education packages are available but do not appear to have undergone any systematic evaluation. It may be that an educational approach which reduces the misuse of tobacco and illicit drugs is not equally effective for alcohol. In addition to making a distinction between educational approaches and underlying models of health-related behaviour, it may also be necessary to distinguish between substances. This is particularly true in a school setting, where the substance may well determine the overall objectives. Thus a school-based illicit drugs education programme is likely to have an ultimate goal of total prevention, whereas alcohol education may focus on harm minimisation or risk reduction. Some of these issues were examined in a recent American study which evaluated a multiple substance abuse programme amongst seventh grade students (12- to 13-year-olds). In this sophisticated study using rigorous methodology, Hansen, *et al.* (1988), compared the effectiveness of two educational approaches – a social influences approach and an affective approach. The social influences programme incorporated many of the ideas discussed above, focusing on influences on substance use such as peer group and other social pressures. The affective programme emphasised 'person-centred' influences and included references to enhancement of self-esteem, decision-making, stress management and more general 'coping skills'. Overall the results of this study indicated the superiority of the social influences approach in preventing the onset of substance use. There was even some indication that the affective education had increased the risk of experimentation. This latter finding led the authors to speculate that the affective education may have presented an unintended message that psychoactive substances can help with coping skills. The social influences approach alone appeared to have been effective in reducing existing levels of consumption, although this was not significant for all three substances. This investigation clearly demonstrates that different educational approaches may result in a different outcome for different substances, in this case alcohol, tobacco and cannabis/marijuana.

In conclusion, it would appear that broad generalisations cannot be made about how to educate young people effectively about psychoactive drug use. All such educational initiatives must at some point differentiate between substance, programme goals and educational rationale. This is especially important for the purposes of evaluation. So where do we go from here? Goodstadt (1986) has reiterated the general ineffectiveness of drugs education programmes, especially in North America. As many other commentators, this author has also lamented the absence of careful evaluation methodology. But rather than provide further reviews of the somewhat depressing evidence, he has tried to identify some of the reasons for repeated failure to provide evidence of effectiveness with a view to recommending future strategies. The difficulty of building on what has gone before in the field of drugs education is emphasised, and is attributed largely to consistently negative findings on effectiveness. Goodstadt has also noted that while some of the more positive outcomes have been associated with increased knowledge, this on its own is insufficient to bring about the intended change in substance-related behaviour, arguing that attitudes and beliefs also have a role to play in achieving behavioural change. His recommendations include greater attention to the implementation of drugs education initiatives. Careful consideration should be given to the process of implementation, addressing such issues as teacher readiness or time allocation, and to the sequence of introduction into the curriculum, especially in terms of links with other subjects already being taught. He has argued strongly that such programmes must include time 'for the development, rehearsal and reinforcement of newly acquired skills and behaviours' (Goodstadt 1986: 280). The need for careful evaluation is also stressed.

Educating young people about drugs is a complex issue which should not be oversimplified. It should already be clear from this chapter that the way in which young people use and misuse alcohol, tobacco and illicit drugs cannot be regarded in isolation from the more general developmental trends and problems of adolescence.

Although some association has been identified between the misuse of alcohol and other drugs (Plant, *et al.* 1985; Bagnall 1988), there is no firm or consistent evidence that drinking behaviour during adolescence accurately predicts subsequent adult drinking behaviour. Nevertheless, a longitudinal study in Britain of alcohol consumption at the ages of 16 and 23 suggested that those who drank most and more frequently at 16 were the most likely to drink heavily at 23 (Ghodsian and Power 1987). Furthermore, it has been argued that early drinking habits may affect the physiological and psychological maturation of the individual (Gordon and McAlister 1982). The role of adolescent skills in drugs education has been noted: 'The objectives related to substance abuse prevention converge with promoting healthy adolescent development; building a society in which people are educated to care more effectively for themselves and for one another' (McAlister 1982: 169). The dangers of isolating substance use from the wider issues of adolescence have also been acknowledged by Petersen (1982) who advocated knowledge about adolescent development as a basic prerequisite for any interventions with adolescent health behaviour. Adolescents, she has argued, must be viewed as whole people, not merely as smokers, drinkers or eaters. If the latter classification is used, there is a danger that appropriate intervention programmes would simply be 'anti-smoking' or 'anti-drinking' programmes, perhaps even originally developed for adults. Such an approach, it is argued, fails to take account of the unique circumstances of adolescence which contribute to health-related behaviours such as smoking and drinking.

However, as noted above, there has to be a point in educating young people about substance misuse when some distinction is made between different psychoactive substances. This is especially true in alcohol education where the prevention of initiation is not always the ultimate goal, but rather the maintenance of health-related behaviour.

This distinction is addressed by Jessor, who argued that:

> The available evidence suggests there is, in fact, no discontinuity between initiation and later phases of involvement, and that different theories (for example, maladjustment or some form of psychopathology) are not needed to account for heavy involvement as against moderate involvement or even initiation.
>
> (Jessor 1982: 460)

However, he did also concede that there is a need for further research to clarify and possibly even settle this issue. High research priority is also recommended in the context of prevention by means of health education, particularly to explore the effectiveness of interventions which combine what Jessor terms a 'specific behaviour approach' and a 'whole person approach'. The former concerns skills specific to the substance in question, such as resistance to peer group pressure in smoking tobacco or consuming alcohol. The unkown quantity in this approach is the extent to which skills relating to one specific substance will be transferable to different contexts. The second approach is more general and focuses on *central* change in individuals, such as self-esteem or self-identity, which are assumed to have wide generalised application. The question mark over this approach is whether the broad generalisation of application has any significant influence on specific behaviours. A strategy which combines these two approaches is intuitively appealing since each should counteract the inherent weakness of the other. It is this combined approach which Jessor sees as deserving of high research priority.

An approach of this kind to educating young people about drugs misuse would clearly encompass many of the recommendations arising from the discussion in this chapter. At the same time, it would go some way to addressing some of the acknowledged problems and pitfalls.

Finally, a brief word must be said about the alcohol education project described in the remainder of this book, and its theoretical stance in relation to the above discussions. The teaching package evaluated in the study specifically addressed alcohol misuse amongst 12- to 13-year-olds, and was therefore substance specific. However, it was designed in a way which should enable it to be readily integrated into an overall health education programme, especially one which acknowledges some of the more general problems of adolescence. In this context it could be described as an example of the combined approach recommended by Jessor. The rationale underlying the specific teaching package devised for this study will be explained in detail in Chapter 4. Meanwhile, Chapters 2 and 3 will focus on the evaluation method, and some of the preliminary findings resulting from the baseline survey.

Chapter 2
The research

This book describes a research project undertaken between March 1986 and March 1989. The main objective of the study, as noted above, was to evaluate the effectiveness of a school-based alcohol education programme for 12- and 13-year-olds. The project followed on logically from an earlier Alcohol Research Group study of teenagers in the Lothian region of Scotland. This earlier exercise had involved a questionnaire survey of young people at two points in time – first in 1979 and 1980 when the study group were 15 to 16 years old and again in 1983 and 1984 when they were 19 to 20 years old. The questionnaires elicited data on the pattern of use of alcohol, tobacco and illicit drugs amongst these young people. The primary component of the study was to determine for this population whether knowledge, attitudes and behaviour concerning alcohol predicted subsequent alcohol- (or other drug-) related behaviour. The findings have been described in Plant, *et al.* (1985) and will not be repeated here, other than to note that direct prediction did not seem possible. There was very little association between alcohol consumption at the age of 15 to 16 and four years later. However, two points from the concluding chapter of that publication are highly relevant to the present book. In the context of alcohol education, one of the authors had noted in an earlier publication that 'alcohol education has been promoted above all other methods of primary prevention despite no evidence to show that it works' (Samuel, 1984: 1). However, in their conclusions, the authors have argued that:

> It would be totally unjustified on the basis of current evidence to discard education as a response to youthful . . . substance misuse. . . . Further initiatives need to be conducted with care and on an experimental basis. Aims and methods need to be selected,

following the guidance of available world-wide evidence. Evaluation must be taken seriously and should be conducted with openness and rigour.

(Plant *et al.* 1985: 119)

THE PILOT STUDY

In the light of such recommendations, the Alcohol Research Group conducted a pilot study to assess what teachers and educational administrators regard as the important features of a worthwhile alcohol education programme. In 1983 a postal survey was carried out in all local education authorities in the United Kingdom, and 125 questionnaires were returned. Overall a favourable attitude emerged towards alcohol education in the secondary school syllabus, with 99 per cent of respondents expressing willingness to implement any new and useful approach to the subject. The major objectives of any such education were perceived to be changes in information (70.6 per cent of respondents), in attitudes (97.8 per cent) and in drinking habits (62.0 per cent). The survey also indicated that for any alcohol education package to be of practical value, it must satisfy certain basic, if somewhat idealistic criteria. It must be:

> easy to use and not too long
> relevant to the target population
> readily integrated into the existing curriculum
> inexpensive (ideally free)
> developed in close co-operation with experienced teachers

Armed with this information, the Alcohol Research Group was in a strong position to develop an alcohol education programme. This would take account, not just of what had been effective in the past, but also of the needs of the potential consumers, that is, the teachers and other educationalists who would take part in developing and implementing the programme. It is emphasised that the five practical constraints noted above made it unlikely that dramatic results would be achieved by the resultant alcohol education programme.

THE MAIN STUDY

The principal aim of the main study was to conduct a systematic evaluation of the effectiveness of an alcohol education package specially developed for 12- to 13-year-olds in schools.

The effectiveness would be measured in terms of changes in the knowledge, attitudes and behaviour of the study group in relation to alcohol.

The educational rationale underlying the package would incorporate evidence on effective approaches from other evaluation studies throughout the world. In addition, the package developed would aim to satisfy the five basic criteria above.

THE STUDY AREAS

The study was conducted in state schools in three regions of Britain. Because the primary focus of the study was to examine changes over time in the same population, a nationally representative sample was not required, and would have necessitated a much larger and more costly exercise. The three regions were selected as a result of the pilot study for two main reasons: they had expressed a strong desire to be actively involved in any subsequent research, and to allow representation of one local education authority from each of England, Scotland and Wales.

The three areas finally selected were Berkshire in England, the Highland region in Scotland and Dyfed in Wales, as illustrated in Figure 2.1.

The socio-economic characteristics of these three regions are shown in Table 2.1.

Table 2.1 Unemployment rate by local authority districts at time of surveys

Region	Unemployment rate	
	1986	*1988*
Dyfed	16.6	15.5
Berkshire	6.7	4.1
Highland	16.1	15.2

THE STUDY DESIGN

A prospective design was adopted. The overall research had three principal stages:

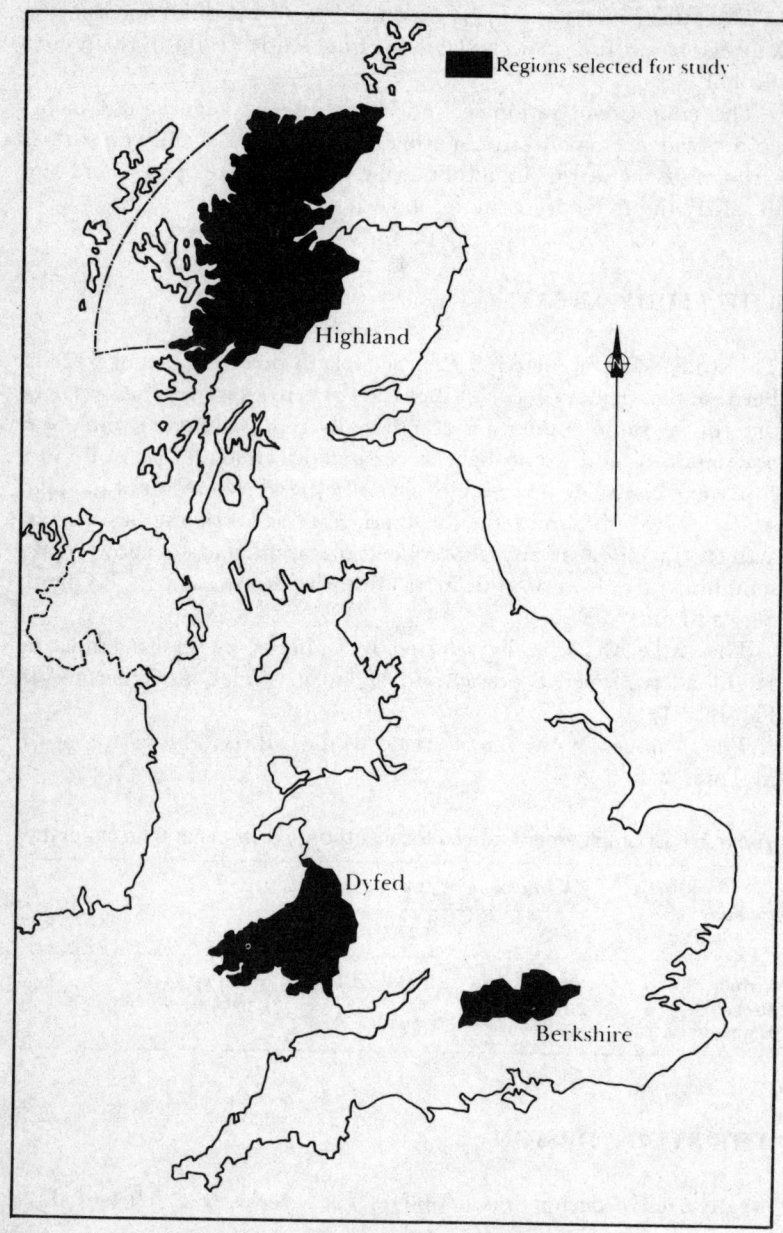

Figure 2.1 Map of Britain to show the position of three regions selected for study

Baseline survey

A questionnaire was completed by all 12- to 13-year-olds in the selected schools. This was designed to elicit data on alcohol-related knowledge, attitudes and behaviour of the complete study group.

Development and administration of the alcohol education package

The first school in each region had no involvement in the development of the educational materials. Class teachers in these schools were asked to teach the package after a 30 minute introduction. The second school from each region seconded two specialist teachers for a short period to assist with the development of the package. These teachers were then responsible for teaching the package to all their second-year pupils. The third school in each region had no exposure to the alcohol education, and acted as a control.

Follow-up survey

This entailed readministration of the questionnaire to the complete study group in all the selected schools approximately fifteen months after completion of the educational intervention.

The main purpose of the study was to analyse the shift in knowledge, attitudes and behaviour between baseline and follow-up surveys. Comparison between control and intervention group schools would give an indication of the effectiveness of the alcohol education package.

This research design is illustrated in Figure 2.2.

It can be seen that the project had two main strands:

(a) questionnaire surveys of alcohol-related knowledge, attitudes and behaviour of the study group;
(b) development and administration of an alcohol education package.

SELECTION OF SCHOOLS

The co-operation of directors of education in each regional authority was secured by personal visits, at which the details of school involvement were discussed. Three schools were required from each region,

36 Educating young drinkers

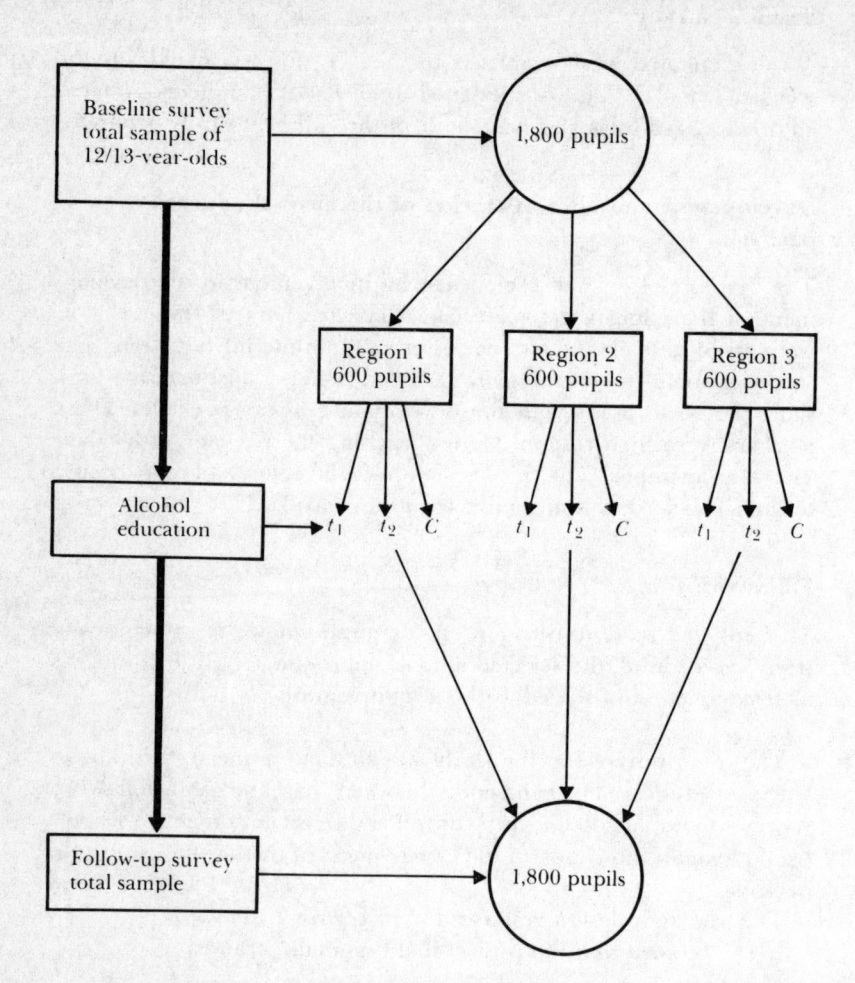

t_1 group...alcohol education package administered by 'uninitiated' class teacher
t_2 group...alcohol education package administered by 'specialist' teacher from own school
C group... control group, with no exposure to the alcohol education package

Figure 2.2 Detailed research design

all of which would take part in the questionnaire surveys. Nine schools were selected to participate in this study. For the purposes of evaluation, one school in each region would act as a control, and would have no exposure to the alcohol education materials. It was therefore important that the control schools were geographically distant from the others in the study, to avoid 'contamination'. The major constraint in selection of the other two (intervention group) schools in each region was that the staff (or at least the headteacher) must have some commitment to providing alcohol education. In addition the 'specialist' intervention school (t_2 group in Figure 2.2) had to be willing to co-opt one or two experienced health or social education teacher(s) to work with the author in developing the educational materials. Otherwise the schools selected with the assistance of directors of education and senior advisors were chosen to represent a mixed 'catchment area' population. Three state comprehensive schools satisfying these criteria were selected from each region, giving a total of nine schools.

Headteachers of individual schools were approached initially by senior advisers in their regions and then contacted personally by the author to discuss detailed requirements. At this stage two schools had to be replaced – one because it was too small to give the necessary quota, and another because it was already very actively involved in its own alcohol education programme.

Selection bias within schools was avoided by including in the study all children aged 12 to 13 years in each school.

In advance of the survey, copies of a standardised letter were sent to each school for circulation to the parents of all potential respondents. This letter outlined the research project, reassured parents of confidentiality and gave them the option to withdraw their children from participation if so desired. This 'contracting out' option follows a procedure elaborated in the earlier Lothian region survey referred to above. Only 3.4 per cent of potential respondents withdrew in this way, the numbers therefore being too small to merit collection of independent data on this group. In addition, comments from school staff indicated that the pupils who did withdraw did not appear to differ conspicuously from the participants in terms of academic ability or home environment. The resulting study group contained 1,586 pupils, approximately 500 per region. The male:female ratio for each region was similar, with approximately equal numbers of either sex being included in the study. The mean age for the total study group was 13 years 1 month. The distribution of age and sex by region is shown in Table 2.2.

Table 2.2 Regional distribution of age and sex

	Highland	Berkshire	Dyfed	Total study group
Total *n*	576	609	401	1,586
n – males	290 (50.3%)	315 (51.7%)	207 (51.6%)	812 (51.2%)
n – females	286 (49.7%)	294 (48.3%)	194 (48.4%)	774 (48.8%)
Average age (mode)	13yrs 6mths	13yrs 2mths	12yrs 9mths	12yrs 11mths

SURVEY INSTRUMENT

Data collection was by self-completed questionnaire, administered in a group setting. The questionnaire was adapted from the one used by Plant, *et al.* (1985) in their survey of 15- and 16-year-olds in the Lothian region of Scotland. The principal changes required to adapt the earlier instrument for the present study involved simplifying the language for this younger age group and removing questions clearly not relevant to 12- to-13-year-olds. The revised questionnaire was pre-tested on four 13-year-olds, and piloted on approximately 150 second-year pupils in two large Edinburgh state comprehensive schools. This indicated one further important revision, when many of these pupils were unable to complete the section on attitudes which was presented in a five-point rating scale format. This was replaced by a set of twenty attitude statements, to which pupils responded either 'agree', 'disagree' or 'not sure'. The questionnaire elicited information on biographical details, factual knowledge and experience of, and attitudes towards alcohol and its consequences, together with data on the use of tobacco and illicit drugs. The questionnaire is reproduced in Appendix 1(a). A Welsh language version (Appendix 1(b)) is also included: this was required for the control group school in Dyfed, which is a Welsh-speaking school.

Some reservations are often expressed about the reliability and validity of self-reported survey data (for example, Pernanen 1974; Marsh, *et al.* 1986; Crawford 1987). The decision in this study to elicit such data in a school setting was prompted by several factors. Perhaps the most important of these is the increased validity over alternative methods such as individual interviewing, with the possibility of interviewer bias, especially in face-to-face interviews with young people in the home setting (McKennel 1980). Furthermore, simultaneous collection of self-reported data enables a larger study group to be surveyed more easily and cheaply than would individual interviewing.

QUESTIONNAIRE ADMINISTRATION

The survey was conducted in individual schools during November and December 1986. Questionnaires were administered in class or larger groups by the author and colleagues, with the assistance of locally-recruited supply teachers. No class teacher was present during questionnaire administration, in order to reassure pupils of confidentiality. In this study anonymity was not possible because of the need to resurvey the same respondents approximately fifteen months later. Two schools, however, were unwilling to participate unless anonymity was guaranteed. Consequently a number was allocated by these schools to each of the pupils involved and this replaced the name on the questionnaire. A record linking these numbers with names had been lodged securely with the local education authority and was accessed only by the school for cross-matching individuals in the follow-up survey. All respondents were provided with written and verbal assurances that their identities would be treated as strictly confidential.

For the Welsh-speaking school in Dyfed, the questionnaires which had been translated into the Welsh language were administered by bilingual supply teachers under the supervision of the author. The responses in Welsh were then translated into English by a Welsh speaker in Edinburgh, prior to computer coding.

DEVELOPMENT OF EDUCATION PACKAGE

Information from the pilot study had indicated that teachers and senior educationalists were not unaware that some good alcohol education material is already available in the United Kingdom. However, these packages are frequently viewed as too expensive for individual schools to purchase, or unrealistically demanding in terms of preparation time and/or in-service training. For the purposes of the present study, it was decided to put together, selecting appropriately from existing materials, a package which overcomes some of these difficulties and thus aims to satisfy the criteria identified in the pilot study.

As noted in Figure 2.2, one school in each region seconded one or two teacher(s) to assist with development of the alcohol education materials. Five teachers subsequently attended a two-day workshop organised in Edinburgh, with the objective of drawing up a framework for the package content. Although the academic backgrounds of these teachers were varied, they were all highly experienced in personal and social/health education or guidance. The author maintained contact with these five teachers by personal visits during the detailed development of the alcohol education materials. The resulting package was piloted on approximately 600 second-year pupils with seventeen teachers in three state comprehensive schools in the Lothian region. Modifications recommended by the piloting were incorporated into the final version of the package used for evaluation.

The timetable for the complete three-year study is shown below.

Timetable of three-year study

1. *March – July 1986*
   Initial contacts made with the three study areas.
   Survey questionnaire devised.
2. *August – September 1986*
   Package prepared for piloting following two-day workshop with co-opted teachers.
   Questionnaire piloted in Lothian region schools.
3. *October 1986 – March 1987*
   Baseline survey conducted in three regions.
   Education package piloted in Lothian region schools.
4. *April – June 1987*
   Package taught in study group schools.
5. *July 1987 – March 1988*
   Analysis of baseline data.
6. *April – May 1988*
   Follow-up survey conducted in three regions.
7. *June 1988 – March 1989*
   Analysis and documentation of survey results.

Chapter 3
The baseline survey

As noted in Chapter 2, all pupils in the study group completed a survey questionnaire at the start of the research project. Details of this questionnaire are included in Appendix 1(a). It will be remembered that this instrument was translated into Welsh for use in Dyfed – the Welsh language version is included in Appendix 1(b). The aim of the questionnaire was to give an indication of the knowledge, attitudes and behaviour of those young people in relation to alcohol. This 'baseline' measure was taken from all pupils in the study *before* the pupils in the two intervention groups received the alcohol education package. The questionnaire survey was repeated on the study group approximately fifteen months after the baseline survey. During the intervening period the pupils in the two intervention groups had been taught the alcohol education package. Those in the control or comparison group schools did not have any alcohol education. The differences which occurred between the first and second surveys will be discussed in detail in Chapter 6; these findings constitute the basis of the evaluation in question. This chapter will concentrate on the findings of the baseline survey, before any of the study group were exposed to the alcohol education package being evaluated.

Emphasis will be placed here on the descriptive findings of the baseline survey. This will keep statistical technicalities to a minimum, and should help to paint a broad picture of how this group of 12- to 13-year-olds use (and misuse) alcohol, how much they know about it and how they feel about it.

The distribution of age and sex of the 1,586 respondents in the baseline survey for each of the three regions was illustrated in Table 2.2 of Chapter 2.

An important point to note here is that the study group used in this research was not selected by a technique which would produce a sample which was statistically representative of the total population of 12- to 13-year-olds in Britain. Consequently, the picture of the study group described in this chapter would not necessarily be the same for all comparable groups in British schools. A nationally representative sample was not required for this study since the evaluation was based on changes within the same group of young people. It does, however, limit the extent to which the findings can be extended beyond this particular group of 12- to 13-year-olds.

The next few pages will build up a picture of the study group and alcohol. Comparisons will then be made with other similar surveys, and it will be noted that, despite the sampling limitations noted above, this study group was not remarkably different from its counterparts in more representative studies.

RESULTS

Experience of alcohol

Ninety-six per cent of all 12- to 13-year-olds in the baseline survey reported having tasted an alcoholic drink. Four per cent were thus abstainers. The most common age for first taste of alcohol was 11 to 12 years. Parents or adults other than parents were reported as the providers of the first taste of alcohol for 81 per cent of the study group. For 84 per cent the first taste occurred in the family home.

The principal measure of alcohol consumption in this survey referred to the last occasion on which respondents had consumed alcohol. This is in contrast with many other surveys, particularly those of older respondents, which generally use a 'seven-day diary'. As the name suggests, this is intended to help the respondent to provide a detailed account of the amount of alcohol consumed on each of the seven days prior to the survey. However, a previous survey of teenagers (Plant, *et al.* 1985) had indicated that only a minority of 15- to 16-year-olds reported drinking alcohol every week. Moreover, when the survey questionnaire for the present study was piloted with a seven-day diary included it became clear that very few of the 12- to 13-year-old respondents had consumed any alcohol in the preceding seven days. A measure of alcohol consumption based on this technique therefore appeared of little value, since most youngsters would not be able to provide any information. In the main study then, respondents were asked when they had last consumed alcohol, how much they had consumed, and who they were with on this occasion. Fifteen per cent reported that they had drunk alcohol in the last seven days, while 37 per cent report not having done so for more than twelve weeks.

Seventy-three per cent of respondents reported that they had been with their parents on this last occasion, and 20 per cent said they had been with friends of the same age.

Figure 3.1 illustrates the amounts of alcohol which respondents reported they had consumed on the last occasion. These quantitites are subdivided into three categories of alcohol type – beers (this includes ciders), wines (this includes fortified wine such as sherry) and spirits.

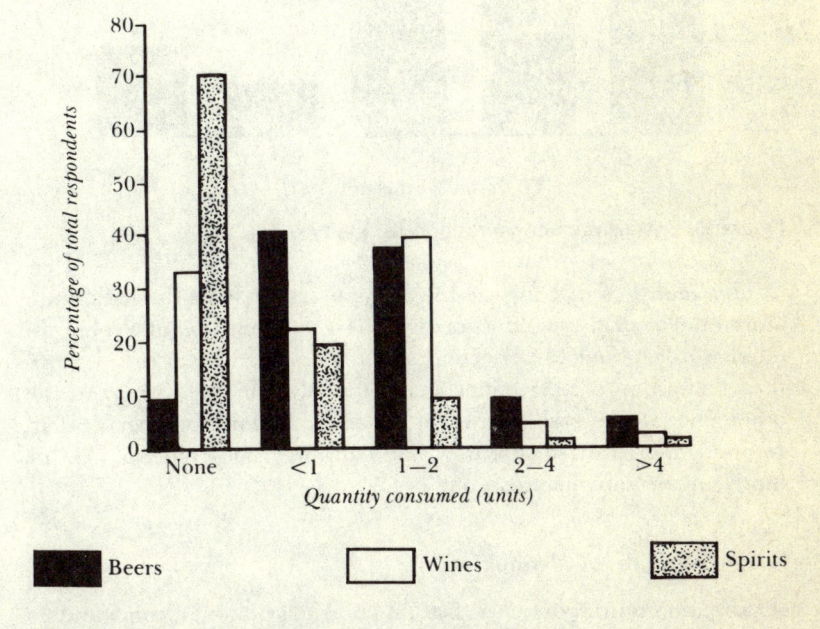

Figure 3.1 Quantity consumed on last occasion

Two points emerge from Figure 3.1. First, few of the young people in this study had consumed more than four units of alcohol on the last occasion. This is equivalent to two pints of beer or its equivalent.[1] Second, experience of spirits consumption appeared very limited, with beers (this includes ciders) being the most popular beverage.

Figure 3.2 shows the most alcohol respondents reported that they had ever consumed on one occasion of drinking alcohol.

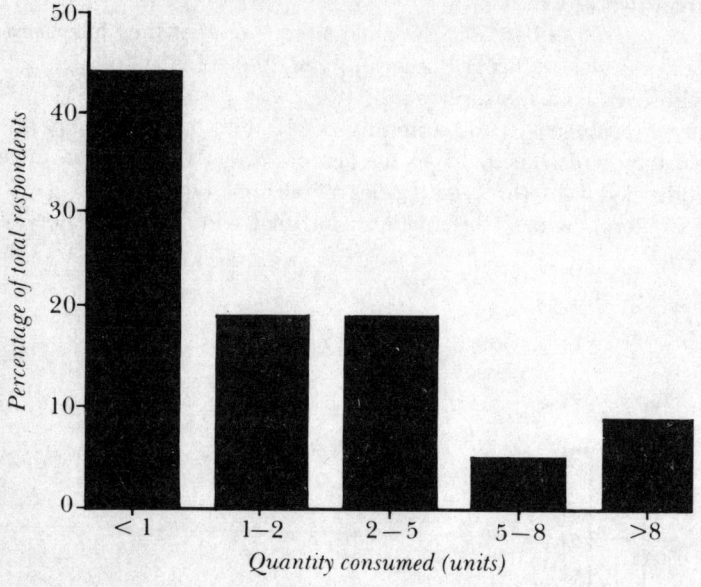

Figure 3.2 Maximum consumption for study group

This indicates that for the majority of respondents the maximum amount of alcohol ever consumed was less than one unit of alcohol. In other words, about 43 per cent of respondents had never drunk more than half a pint of beer, cider or its equivalent in one sitting. At the other end of the scale, however, a small minority, 9 per cent of respondents, reported that they had consumed four pints of beer or more, or its equivalent, on one occasion.

Knowledge about alcohol

Information on respondents' factual knowledge about alcohol and its effects was obtained using a 'quiz' of fifteen statements about alcohol such as, for example, 'Alcohol is a drug'. Full details can be found in Appendix 1. Pupils had to indicate whether they thought each statement was TRUE or FALSE, or whether they did not know the correct answer. In this baseline survey, the most common 'score', that is, total number of items correct on the knowledge quiz, was six out of a possible fifteen. It is interesting to note how unsure the young respondents were about these alcohol-related 'facts'. The most common 'score' for items incorrect was four out of fifteen. As these quiz 'scores' suggest, many respondents chose to tick the 'don't know' option on the knowledge quiz. Analysis of individual items revealed some useful details about the existing knowledge 'base' for this group of young people. Eighty-nine per cent knew that it can be dangerous to drink alcohol if one has taken tablets or medicine, while 69 per cent knew that alcohol is a drug. Fifty-eight per cent agreed that giving alcohol to accident victims may be dangerous.

Conversely, 60 per cent of youngsters wrongly reported that a single whisky (one unit of alcohol) is stronger than a pint of beer (two units), and 77 per cent thought that alcohol makes one more alert. The popular myth that drinking spirits is more likely to lead to problems with alcohol than drinking cider was endorsed by 61 per cent of the study group. This is a worrying finding in that it reinforces the idea that young people (and probably many adults also) do not appreciate the alcoholic strength of cider. In conjunction with its 'sweeter' taste, which is more acceptable to the inexperienced palate than many beers, cider may thus be more open to innocent misuse.

No significant association was found between knowledge about alcohol and variables such as school, sex, socio-economic status or father's current employment status.

Ill-effects of alcohol

Three hundred respondents (20 per cent of the study group) reported having had a hangover. For most this had been experienced only once, with only 14 per cent (1 per cent of the study group) reporting more than four hangovers in the last six months.

Approximately 5 per cent reported some adverse consequence arising from their consumption of alcohol, such as trouble with parents or at school. Twenty-seven per cent reported having had an upset stomach because of drinking and seventy youngsters (4 per cent) had experienced some kind of alcohol-related accident or injury. Drinking alcohol had been a source of worry for 9 per cent of respondents and 13 per cent reported having felt guilty or ashamed about their drinking.

Attitudes about alcohol

A list of twenty short statements about alcohol was devised. Half of these statements were intended to reflect approval of alcohol consumption, for example, 'Alcohol makes people more fun to be with'. The other ten statements were intended to reflect disapproval, for example, 'Young people who drink alcohol are more likely to get into trouble at school'. Once again, full details of these questions can be found in Appendix 1.

Respondents were asked to tick a box to indicate whether they agreed with each statement, whether they disagreed, or whether they were uncertain either way. Agreement with a statement reflecting approval of alcohol consumption was taken to indicate a positive attitude. Disagreement with this statement would be interpreted as a negative attitude. In the same way, agreement with a statement suggesting disapproval of alcohol was interpreted as a negative attitude to alcohol. Disagreement with such a statement was seen to indicate a positive attitude. Using this interpretive framework, it was possible to add up a positive attitude score and a negative attitude score for each respondent.

The average totals for positive and negative attitudes respectively were 3.7 for attitudes favouring alcohol, and 12.4 for attitudes disapproving of it. The maximum possible score for each was 20. As with the items about alcohol-related knowledge, many of the young respondents ticked the options indicating uncertainty. It would thus appear that at the time of the baseline survey, before the alcohol educational intervention, the respondents as a group were more likely to hold attitudes of disapproval towards alcohol.

Perceived parental attitudes to youthful alcohol consumption were also investigated. Forty-three per cent of respondents reported that their father/step-father would object to their drinking alcohol. Fifty per cent thought their mother/step-mother would object. On the other hand, 40 per cent had been offered alcohol to drink by their father/step-father and 30 per cent by their mother/step-mother.

Alcohol education

As noted in the Introduction, alcohol education is generally given very low priority in the school curriculum with no compulsory inclusion in the education system either in England and Wales or in Scotland. This was reinforced by the finding from the baseline survey, where it became clear that provision of school-based alcohol education as indicated by the respondents was minimal in all of the nine schools included in the study. Only 20 per cent of the complete study group recalled having been shown a film or given a leaflet about alcohol. Outside school, several sources of information about alcohol were reported. These were: parents (66 per cent); television or radio (51 per cent); magazines or newspapers (31 per cent) and grandparents (22 per cent). Of particular interest to this evaluation study, no significant association was found between current knowledge about alcohol as assessed by the 'quiz' items and any previous alcohol education. This suggests that any alcohol education which had taken place had had little impact on respondents' knowledge about alcohol.

Tobacco and illicit drugs

The questionnaire survey also asked the young respondents about their use of tobacco and of illicit drugs (not prescribed by a doctor for medical reasons). Thirty-four per cent claimed that they had never smoked tobacco and 6 per cent reported that they currently smoke cigarettes (that is, at the time of the baseline survey). Only 5 per cent of these 12- to 13-year-olds reported having used illicit drugs such as cannabis, glues or solvents. Because of this low incidence it is more informative to look at actual numbers using each drug rather than percentages. These are shown in Table 3.1.

Table 3.1 Illicit drug use for total sample ($n = 1,586$)

Drug	Number responding 'yes'
Cannabis	14
LSD	3
Barbiturates	3
Glues or solvents	30
Amphetamines	6
Opium	2
Morphine	2
Heroin	4
Cocaine	1
Sleeping tablets/tranquillisers	38

Sleeping tablets/tranquillisers were clearly the most commonly used illicit drugs. In view of this, it is important to note that the questionnaire specifically excluded drugs prescribed by a doctor in the relevant question. The misuse of sleeping tablets/tranquillisers referred to here may well have arisen through access to drugs prescribed for someone else, perhaps a parent or relative in the same household as the respondent.

The association between use of illicit drugs and use of alcohol and tobacco was examined. Respondents who reported having used any illicit drug were significantly[2] more likely to have first tasted alcohol at an earlier age. This group was also more likely to have smoked tobacco although there was no difference in current tobacco use between those who had and those who had not used any illicit drug.

SEX DIFFERENCES

Many surveys both in the United Kingdom and in other countries throughout the world have shown large differences between adolescent males and females in their use and misuse of alcohol.

In this study too, analyses were carried out to examine differences between males and females in the study group. Some of the differences which did emerge are discussed below. These were all significant unless otherwise indicated.

Experience of alcohol

Quantity

Several questions in the survey asked the young respondents about the amount of alcohol consumed. In most of these questions the males reported significantly higher levels of consumption than did the females. The trend is illustrated for amount of beer drunk on last occasion in Figure 3.3a, amount of wine drunk on last occasion in Figure 3.3b and most alcohol ever consumed on one single occasion in Figure 3.3c.

Frequency

Respondents were asked when they last had any alcohol to drink; the responses are shown in Figure 3.4.

From this it is clear that males were significantly more likely than females to report having consumed alcohol recently, while females were more likely than males to state that it had been one to three months or more since they had drunk any alcohol. Also, of the 229

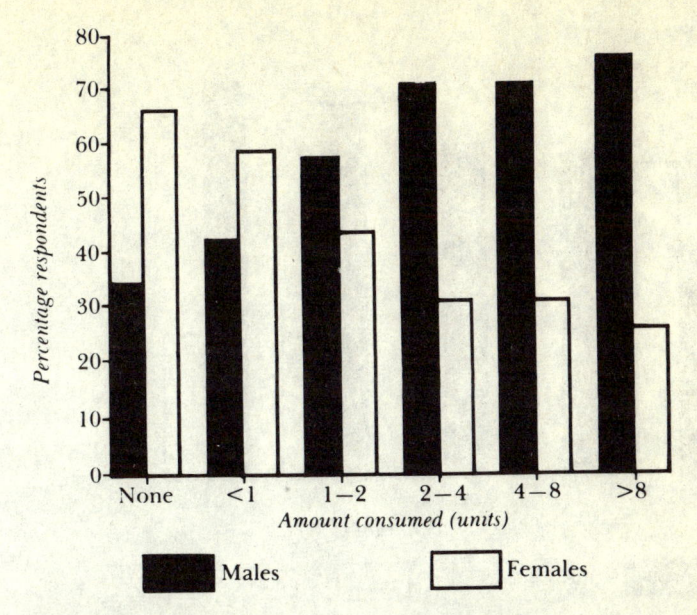

Figure 3.3a Sex differences in beer consumption

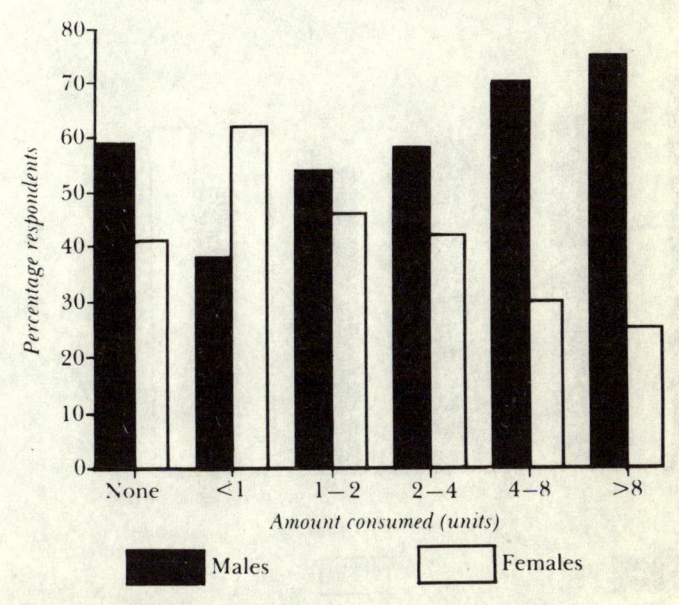

Figure 3.3b Sex differences in wine consumption

50   Educating young drinkers

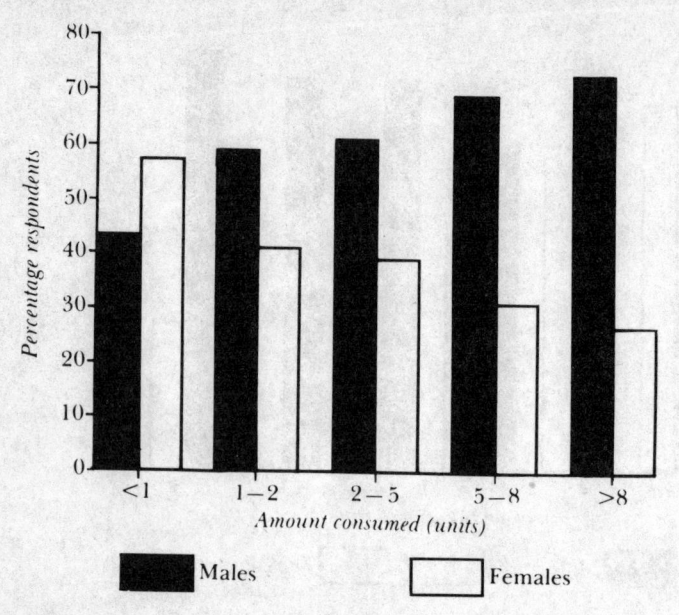

Figure 3.3c   Sex differences in maximum consumption

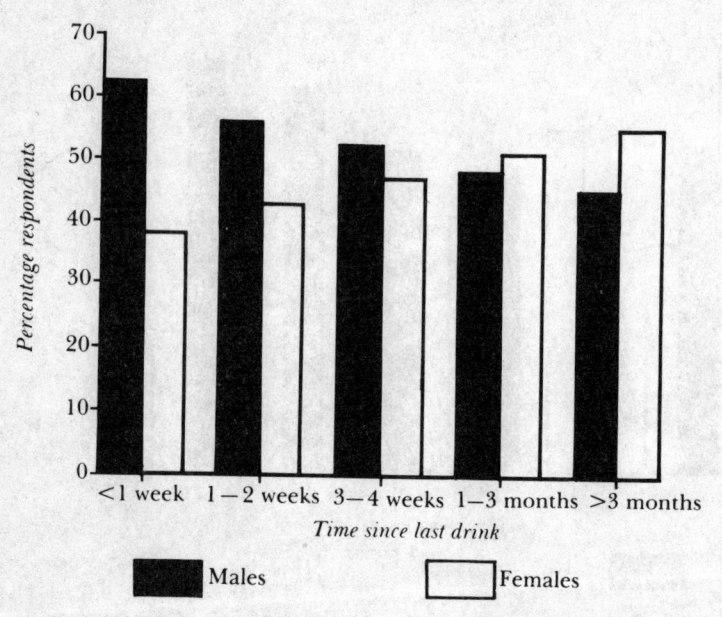

Figure 3.4   Sex differences in frequency of consumption

respondents who reported having consumed alcohol within the last week, 62 per cent were male.

Males were significantly more likely to report having first tasted alcohol at an earlier age than were females. Of those respondents who reported having first tasted alcohol under eight years of age, 57 per cent were males. Males were also more likely than females to have been offered alcohol by their father/step-father. Although only 13 per cent of the study group reported having consumed alcohol outside in a street or a park, 67 per cent of these were males.

Consequences of alcohol consumption

As would be expected from the overall higher consumption of alcohol by males, they also reported more frequent experience of the effects of alcohol, both positive and negative. Although few highly significant sex differences emerged, a clear trend is evident with males more likely to have experienced the effects shown in Table 3.2.

Knowledge about alcohol

The total number of items correct and the total wrong in the knowledge 'quiz' were compared for males and females. Males featured significantly in both categories, that is, males had more items correct than females, but also had more items incorrect. This was explained by the fact that females were more likely than males to select the 'don't know' option. It is only possible to speculate why this should be so. One plausible explanation could be that males are more influenced by social expectations concerning their knowledge about alcohol. In other words, it may not be consistent with a 'macho' image for adolescent males to admit that they do not know specific facts about alcohol. So rather than face a possible loss of image, male adolescents may be more likely than their female counterparts to risk ticking the wrong answer.

Reasons for drinking alcohol

There were some large differences between males and females in the reasons given for drinking alcohol. Males were significantly more likely than females to report that they drank alcohol for the following reasons:

'So as not to be the odd one out'
'To help me mix more easily with other people'
'To help me talk to the opposite sex more easily'
'To look good in front of other people'

These male-dominated explanations appear to reinforce the lack of confidence and concern with image apparently exhibited by male respondents in the questions on alcohol-related knowledge.

Table 3.2 Effects of alcohol consumption more likely to have been experienced by males

Effect	Difference between males and females		
	χ^2	df	p
Feel happy	6.30	2	<0.05
Feel relaxed	7.49	2	<0.05
Feel sick	7.76	2	<0.05
Feel aggressive	13.14	2	<0.01
Feel argumentative	19.34	2	<0.001
Been told off by adults for drinking alcohol	7.58	1	<0.001
Experienced an alcohol-related accident or injury	7.06	1	<0.01
Ever feel guilty about own alcohol consumption	9.01	1	<0.005
Ever had a hangover	4.62	1	<0.05

Notes: χ^2 = chi squared which is the statistic commonly used to test a null hypothesis for two frequencies in alternative categories. In this example, these alternative categories refer to a set of respondents – male and female
df = degrees of freedom
p = probability

Attitudes about alcohol

There were no significant differences between males and females in the study group in their self-reported attitudes about alcohol.

Tobacco and illicit drug use

As noted earlier, the incidence of illicit drug use in this study was too low to allow statistical analyses and comparisons. It was thus not possible to identify any gender differences in illicit drug use.

However, such comparisons were possible on the information about smoking. Although males and females were evenly distributed amongst those who reported that they had ever smoked tobacco, the pattern of smoking behaviour at the time of the survey was significantly different for males and females. These differences are illustrated in Figure 3.5.

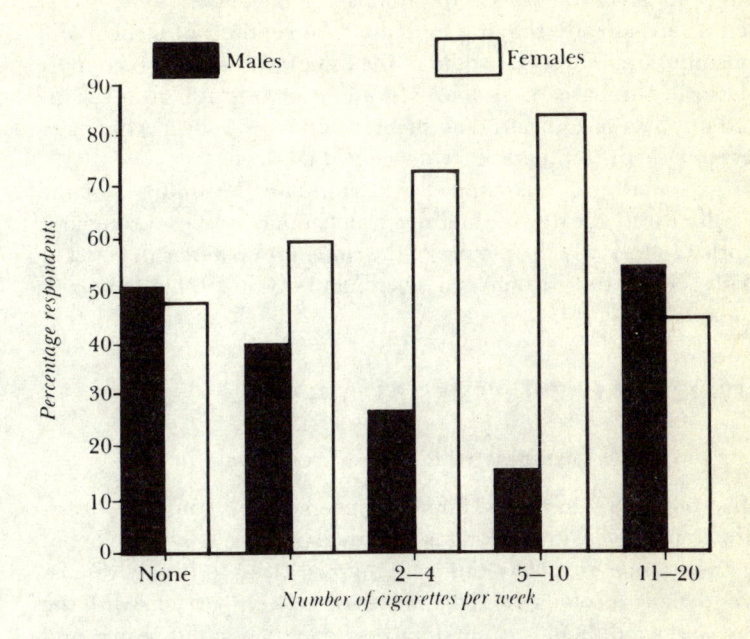

Figure 3.5 Sex differences in current tobacco use

It can be seen that females outnumber males in the categories representing one to ten cigarettes per week. Only when the number of cigarettes per week increases to a figure of eleven to twenty do males overtake females. It should be remembered that the percentages illustrated in Figure 3.5 are taken from a total of 95 respondents, since only 6 per cent of the study group reported that they smoked at the time of survey.

The above findings have painted a picture of the study group which gives some insight into what they know about alcohol, how they use and misuse it, and what they feel about it. In general, the picture suggests that, although most of the 12- to 13-year-olds had some experience of alcohol, it was mostly quite limited, and took place in the family home under parental supervision. However, a small minority of these young people were already misusing alcohol, putting themselves and possibly others at risk of accident and injury. These numbers cannot be ignored, and alone justify some kind of response. Furthermore the young people in the study demonstrated a very limited knowledge about alcohol and its effects. In addition there is some indication, especially amongst the males, that social influences are already shaping individual perceptions of alcohol and its consumption. These are some of the important issues which must clearly form the basis of alcohol education for this age group. This and other surveys indicate that such issues are wholly pertinent to adolescents in Britain and other developed countries.

The remainder of this chapter will compare the findings of the survey discussed above with findings from similar studies throughout the world. In this way the picture of the study group here can be set in a broader context of Britain as a whole, and of some other countries throughout the world.

COMPARISON WITH OTHER STUDIES

Proportion of 13-year-olds who have never tasted alcohol

As Ahlström (1987) has noted for young people in Finland, the transition from abstinence to drinking is a gradual process. It is therefore of great importance to specify the age group referred to in any discussion of juvenile alcohol use. This makes direct comparisons with the present survey difficult as not many studies of young people and alcohol include respondents as young as 13 years.

In their study of 15- to 16-year-olds in the Lothian region of Scotland, Plant, *et al.* (1985) found that 2 per cent were abstainers. Despite the age difference of their study group, a similar figure emerged in the present study of 12- to 13-year-olds, with 4 per cent never having tasted alcohol. This differs from the findings of Marsh, *et al.* (1986) in their national survey of British 13- to 17-year-olds. They found that 6 per cent of 13-year-olds in England and Wales reported that they had never tasted alcohol. In Scotland the corresponding figure was higher with 12 per cent being abstainers. One explanation for this difference between the two studies lies in the nature of the two samples. The study group in the education project, as already noted, was not selected as being representative of the general population. The national survey of Marsh, *et al.* was, however, selected on this basis, in order to enable generalisation of their results to the population of 13- to 17-year-olds in Britain as a whole. Different sample characteristics can bias data. However, as will shortly become apparent, many of the findings in the present study resemble those from other relevant studies. This would suggest that the study group who participated in the alcohol education project did not differ radically from the general population of 12- to 13-year-olds in Britain. A simpler but perhaps more tangible explanation lies in the way questions are worded in different surveys. For instance, in the present study the question under discussion asked: 'Have you ever tasted an alcoholic drink, even just a sip?'. The national survey omitted 'even just a sip'. With this qualification missing it seems quite plausible that fewer respondents would be able to answer 'Yes'. In other words, a high percentage of young people will have tasted a sip of alcohol, but without having had what they regard as an alcoholic drink. It is difficult to overcome ambiguities of this kind in surveys, especially when the respondents have to read the questions and fill in the answers by themselves. The problem of interpreting such questions has been discussed by Gordon and McAlister (1982). In particular, these authors identify the difficulties of comparing surveys which arise from the absence of a uniform definition of what constitutes an alcoholic drink. A further illustration of these problems is quoted in their reference to a national study of adolescent drinking in the United States, in which 38 per cent of American 13-year-olds reported that they were abstainers (Johnston, *et al.* 1977). Clearly this is a much higher proportion than either of the above British studies of 13-year-olds, but may simply reinforce the potential ambiguity of questions such as 'Have you ever had a proper alcoholic drink?'.

Age of first taste

Several studies, especially those which cover a wide age range, have identified the effect of differential memory bias – older respondents tending to recall an older age for this first experience. This phenomenon is by no means unique to surveys of alcohol use. The tendency has, however, been clearly illustrated in this particular context by Ahlström (1987), who found that 23- to 24-year-olds in a Finnish study reported that they had begun drinking alcohol at the age of 15 years. Eight years earlier the same respondents, at age 15 to 16, had reported an average age of 12 years. This highlights the importance of comparing findings only within the same age group. However, even when this constraint is imposed, differences are still apparent between the 13-year-olds in the 1986 British national survey, and the 12- to 13-year-olds in the alcohol education study. In both studies, the most commonly quoted age for the first taste of alcohol was between 11 and 12 years. However, when we look at the proportion who reported having their first taste under nine years of age, some differences emerge. In the national survey, 11 per cent of the total sample came into this category. In the alcohol education study, 20 per cent reported having their first taste under nine years. Once again, however, these differences may well have arisen because of the different wording in the respective questionnaires, with the national survey specifically referring to the first taste of 'a proper alcoholic drink'.

In summary, it would appear that 13-year-olds in Britain are more likely than their American counterparts to have tasted alcohol. Furthermore, the 13-year-olds in the alcohol education study were more likely than those in the national survey of British adolescents to have tasted alcohol, and to have first done so at an earlier age. However, for reasons discussed above, these differences must be interpreted with caution.

Context of first taste

In both the alcohol education study and the 1986 national survey of British adolescents, the majority of 12- and 13-year-olds said that they had had their first taste of alcohol in the family home, and in the presence of parents. Comparison with data from other countries indicates that this is a common, but by no means universal, pattern. Recent surveys in the United States also suggest that the first drink usually occurs in the family context (Gordon and McAlister 1982). In contrast, O'Connor (1985) found that Irish youngsters are most likely to have their first drink in the company of friends and generally without the knowledge of parents. In Iceland, too, young people tend to have their first taste of alcohol in the company of friends, outside the family home. This introduction to alcohol usually occurs long before they are offered a drink by their parents (Olafsdottir 1985). Hibbel (1985) indicated that young Swedes usually have their first drink of wine in the company of parents, but have their first drink of spirits in the company of friends. Such variations serve to highlight the importance of the cultural role of alcohol. They also illustrate the extent to which young people conform to the social norms and expectations of their own society.

Frequency of consumption

Few large-scale surveys of adolescent drinking have elicited data for 12- and 13-year-olds on how often they drink alcohol. Once again this limited comparisons with the present alcohol education study. The response in this survey to the question 'when did you last have any alcohol to drink?' indicated that 15 per cent had drunk alcohol in the last week, with similar distribution in the three study areas. The same question was asked in the national survey, with slightly different results. For English and Welsh 13-year-olds, 26 per cent had drunk alcohol in the previous week; the corresponding figure for Scottish 13-year-olds was 17 per cent. Respondents in this latter survey were also asked independently to fill in a diary requesting details about their alcohol consumption during the preceding seven days. It is interesting to note that the findings of the questionnaire differed considerably from those of the seven-day diary. The questionnaire results suggested that these young people drank less often than indicated by the details in the diary. Discrepancies of this kind serve to reinforce the need for cautious comparison of findings, particularly if the information is elicited in different ways.

Sex differences

The differences between 12- to 13-year-old males and females identified in the present study are very similar to those in the British national survey and other relevant studies. Even when comparisons are made internationally, there appears to be a common general trend. This is discussed below.

Age of first taste

In a review of data from twenty-eight countries, Ahlström (1988) concluded that females generally first taste alcohol one year later than males. In the United States, Johnston, *et al.* (1977), in a national survey of high school seniors, found that more American males than females had tried an alcoholic drink by age 14. This pattern of earlier male experience of alcohol is also found in the present study.

Frequency of consumption

As in this study, Marsh, *et al.* (1986), in their national survey, found that 13-year-old males were more likely than their female counterparts to report having consumed alcohol in the previous seven days. This corresponds to the findings of the education study. British surveys of slightly older adolescents suggest this is a gender difference which does not disappear with age (Plant, *et al.* 1985; Marsh, *et al.* 1986). A similar trend is indicated by international data. For example, Ahlström (1987) showed that between 1976 and 1984 in Finland, there was a marked drop in frequency of consumption for 15- to 24-year-olds of both sexes. However, in all age groups females still used alcohol less frequently than males. A similar pattern of differences between males and females was identified amongst high school students in the United States (Johnston, *et al.* 1977).

Effects of alcohol

The questions concerning experience of the effects of alcohol consumption in this study are similar to those used in the 1986 national survey of British 13- to 17-year-olds, and in the follow-up of 15- and 19-year-olds in the Lothian region of Scotland. Once again, similar findings emerge in all three surveys, with males more likely than females to report having experienced negative or unpleasant effects.

Tobacco use

Although it is reassuring to find such a high percentage of both males and females reporting that they do not smoke, there is no justification for complacency. In particular, the trend in female cigarette smoking identified in this study and reported in detail from a nationwide sample by Goddard and Ikin (1987) suggests that adolescent females may be more reluctant than males to abstain. This fact should be considered in future tobacco education initiatives.

Conclusion

In conclusion, the majority of 12- to 13-year-olds in this study would appear to drink alcohol neither frequently nor excessively. Despite this, the effects of intoxication have already been experienced by a considerable proportion of respondents. The results from this study generally agree with those from other surveys of young people and alcohol, although it has to be noted that only a limited number of these surveys include the 12- to 13-year-old age group.

The findings here serve to reinforce the argument that alcohol use and misuse amongst young people is a more serious issue than that of illicit drugs. In addition, an association between alcohol and use of tobacco and illicit drugs is identified. Finally, important implications arise for alcohol education amongst school children. Relevant education must be based on what young people already know about alcohol, what they feel about it and how they use or misuse it. The evidence suggests that for this age group at least, the educational emphasis should be on developing an attitude of responsibility towards the use of alcohol, coupled with information on the strength of alcoholic drinks and an awareness of the risks of even occasional intoxication. Such an approach underlies the alcohol education package developed as part of the evaluation study discussed in this book. Details of the development of the teaching package and a description of its content will form the basis of the next chapter.

NOTES

1. One 'unit' of alcohol is equivalent to half a pint of ordinary beer, lager, stout or cider, or to a single measure of spirits or one glass of wine. Each unit contains approximately 10 ml (7.9 g) of absolute alcohol.
2. In order to make the text comprehensible to readers who are not familiar with statistical procedures, statistical tests results are omitted. When significant associations or differences are cited, these refer to confidence intervals of at least $P < 0.05$, unless otherwise stated. A value of $P < 0.05$ means that the difference in question could be expected to exist by chance less than 1 in 500 times.

Chapter 4

The teaching package

This chapter will concentrate on the alcohol education package which was specially devised for the research study. Details will be given about how the package was developed, piloted and then implemented in the study group schools. The rationale underlying the teaching materials will be considered, as will the role of teachers using the package. These issues will be discussed in relation to health education in general.

The World Health Organization has defined health as 'a state of complete physical, mental and social well-being, not merely the absence of disease and infirmity' (cited in Schools Council/Health Education Council Project, 1984). Such a definition removes the concept of health from an exclusively medical setting, and broadens the issues into the wider community. Stimulated by this approach, the Schools Council/Health Education Council Project (1984) has highlighted the role of the educational sector in providing health education:

> The health problems facing society today are more concerned with individual behaviour or life style than with environmental health and infectious diseases. If we are to promote positive health as well as to prevent ill-health, health education in schools and colleges can contribute much to that endeavour.
> (Schools Council/Health Education Council Project 1984: Introductory Handbook: 1)

The aims of such health education are seen to include: 'Helping young people to determine where they have control over their health and where they can by conscious choices determine their future health and lifestyles'.

Critics of this approach to health education may argue that placing so much emphasis on the individual is little more than a 'victim blaming' approach. But as argued in Chapter 1, education is necessary to stimulate political will. This in turn is ultimately required to bring about change in any society. This may be especially true in the field of health education and subsequent change in health-related behaviour.

DEVELOPING A HEALTH EDUCATION PACKAGE: SOME KEY ISSUES

In developing any health education, it is important to avoid simply producing a miscellaneous collection of resources with no clear overall aims or target group. In the present study, the first step towards producing a school-based alcohol education package was to assess the needs of the potential consumers, that is, the educationalists who would use the materials. This task had identified the need for a short, 'user-friendly' pack with content relevant to the young people for whom it was intended. Bearing this in mind, the next step was to give some consideration to potential difficulties in implementing the alcohol education programme. Before any health education is introduced into a school or college setting, some fundamental issues must be addressed. The most important of these have been clearly set out as a guide to health education co-ordinators in the form of six simple questions (Schools Council/Health Education Council Project 1984). Although this sequence was intended to facilitate the implementation of a programme encompassing all aspects of health education, it was found to be of practical relevance in the developmental phase of the present alcohol education initiative. Because of their usefulness, these guidelines will be considered in some detail here. It is hoped that they may also prove valuable to any readers who are practically involved in developing a school-based health education programme.

These questions ask of the programme to be introduced:

Where?   This refers to the *context* of the implementation, for example, its place within the existing curriculum.
How?   This refers to the *methods* of the implementation, for example, didactic or non-didactic; teacher- or pupil-centred.
What?   This refers to the *content* of the proposed programme, for example, is it primarily problem focused, topic centred, or aims related?

When?   This refers to the *developmental stage* of the proposed target group (and thus raises implications about their readiness for the programme).

For whom?   This refers again to the proposed *target population*, for example, all pupils or some pupils?

By whom?   This refers to *staffing*, for example, will the health education be implemented and taught by specially trained teachers, class teachers with no special training, or outsiders?

The answers to these questions are intended to assist health programme developers to focus on the principal aspects of their programme. The specific answers relating to the alcohol education programme in the present study are outlined below. These should provide some idea of the shape of the proposed intervention.

DEVELOPING THE ALCOHOL EDUCATION PACKAGE

By limiting the topic of health education to alcohol, specific answers to the above questions can serve as useful pointers to the overall content and method of the teaching package. This is illustrated with reference to individual questions as follows:

Context

In one respect alcohol education should have a readily identifiable slot in the curriculum, as a single aspect of more general health education. However, its place within the curriculum is not always clear. For instance, some aspects of alcohol education, such as those concerning chemistry or physiological effects of ethyl alcohol, already fit comfortably into the science curriculum. This, however, would exclude other issues such as social influences on alcohol consumption, which are more relevant to social education.

In the present project it was necessary for the purpose of evaluation to ensure that the alcohol education provided was as similar as practically possible in all participating schools. Early discussions with potential participants indicated that the most acceptable place in the school curriculum would be that of Personal and Social Education in England and Wales, and its equivalent, Guidance, in Scottish schools. (This distinction was required because Scotland has an education system which is wholly independent from that in England and Wales.)

Methods

Since alcohol education is neither a compulsory subject nor one which is formally assessed for individual achievement, a non-didactic approach emphasising pupil participation seemed most appropriate for the present research. This approach frees teachers from the responsibility of appearing as a 'font of all knowledge', particularly important in a context where some of the content may be unfamiliar to the teacher. In addition, activity-based learning focusing on small group work allows pupils to define their own boundaries on the programme content. This in turn enables them to relate the alcohol education to their own personal experience. This educational rationale is broadly in line with the psychological theory of George Kelly as applied to an educational context (Kelly 1970; Bannister and Salmon 1975; Pope and Keen 1981). Kelly's 'personal contruct' theory underlies a recent resource development for the teaching of science in secondary (high) schools in England and Wales (Secondary Science Curriculum Review, 1983), and is implicit in much of the health education material produced for school pupils. Central to Kelly's position is an emphasis on the person as a 'meaning-maker'. In the particular context of health education, it has been noted that 'to be understood and accepted . . . health education needs to relate to the sense people make of their personal experience' (Health Education Studies Unit 1982). As noted in Chapter 1, problem behaviour theory (Jessor and Jessor 1977) stressed the importance of exploring the meanings attached to adolescent behaviours such as smoking or getting drunk. More recently Jessor has argued that:

> What is lacking in much current research on adolescent health-related behaviour is an effort to occupy an *internal* vantage point, to explore the phenomenology of such behaviour from the adolescent's perspective, to see these behaviours in the light of the subjective meaning or function they have for the young person. . . . In the last analysis, those functions, those subjective reasons, and those personal meanings determine whether the behaviours will or will not occur.
>
> (Jessor 1982: 458)

By placing emphasis on individual participation and open-ended activities it was intended that the alcohol education in this study would have relevance for each participant and would be capable of integration into their personal constructions of reality. The method of implementation was therefore intended to be pupil-centred.

Content

The chosen methods in response to question two above, will obviously influence content (and vice versa). The present alcohol education programme is not problem focused, other than in the general sense of considering 'problems' of adolescence (for example, social relationships, peer group pressure, parental attitudes) in the specific context of alcohol. Although this suggests a topic-centred content (that is, alcohol) it was anticipated that some of the cognitive skills acquired would be transferable to other health issues. This, of course, could not be guaranteed, as indicated in Chapter 1. The content was also defined by the collective aims of the alcohol education package, and by the learning outcomes or educational objectives for individual activities.

Developmental stage

As noted earlier, the chosen subjects for this exercise were 12- to 13-year-olds, most likely to be in their second year of secondary education. It is impossible to generalise about the developmental stage of any one age group as there will be considerable variation amongst individuals. This reinforces the appropriateness of pupil participation with its in-built flexibility.

The issue of relevance of content is important here. For instance, in the context of alcohol, the healthy choice for adolescents was agreed to be one which takes account of the risks of intoxication. This was seen to be of much greater relevance for young people than long-term risks of heavy alcohol consumption such as liver cirrhosis.

Target population

As the age limit had already been decided, this question concerned whether the alcohol education programme should be aimed at *all* 12- to 13-year-olds, or only at those who were perceived to be at greater risk. The responses to the preceding questions suggested a target population of all 12- to 13-year-olds. The issue then had to be considered whether the content of the package would be accessible to

12- to 13-year-olds with learning difficulties, and therefore not wholly dependent on academic skills such as reading ability.

Discussions with potential participants resulted in the decision to include 12- to 13-year-olds of all abilities. Consequently, the stimulus material would include pictorial and oral work, as well as written text.

Staffing

In order to adhere to the research design established for this alcohol education project, little flexibility in staffing was possible. All of the school staff who participated in the study were teachers of social education, religious education or guidance. In practice, the headteacher of each school involved had agreed to take part in the research exercise, thus leaving individual teachers with little choice in the matter. In a more 'normal' situation, however, staffing is an important issue in the implementation of health education, and will be considered in the final chapter which considers some of the wider implications of the present study.

As already noted, one of the major innovations and strengths of the alcohol education package was the close co-operation of experienced health/social education teachers in its development. The preliminary content of the package was established during an intensive two-day meeting of those teachers in Edinburgh. The finer details of the package were negotiated by telephone and visits by the author to these teachers in their schools.

THE RESULTING PACKAGE – A DETAILED DESCRIPTION

The alcohol education materials which resulted from this research have been published separately (Bagnall 1990). It is therefore not appropriate to reproduce these materials in their entirety in this book. However, this section will provide a detailed review of the content, the aims of specific activities in the package and the rationale underlying their inclusion.

The manual for teachers

The package comprised a manual for teachers, providing guidelines for classroom administration and detailed learning outcomes for each of the individual pupil activities. In the introduction to this manual, teachers were informed of the overall aims of the package and its rationale.

It was explained that the principal purpose of the package was to help promote responsible use of alcohol amongst young people. It was *not* intended to advise young people that they must *NEVER* drink alcohol. This would have been a wholly unrealistic aim, since fewer than 10 per cent of the adult population in Britain are total abstainers (Royal College of Psychiatrists 1986). This statistic also justifies the argument that alcohol education must at some point in the school health education curriculum be differentiated from 'illicit drugs' education. By definition, illicit drug use involves breaking the law and the school's responsibility is seen as one of preventing such illegal behaviour. However, alcohol consumption amongst the target age group is legal under certain circumstances (such as in the family home), thus making it more acceptable and practical to promote a message of 'harm minimisation' or 'low-risk drinking'.

It was also made clear to participating teachers that the package was undergoing scientific evaluation for a research project, and therefore it was important for teachers to adhere as closely as possible to the guidelines for teaching the materials.

It was acknowledged that such a prescriptive and standardised approach was not likely to be popular, especially in the context of social education. However, it was also made clear that such constraints would only be necessary during the evaluation phase, and that teachers would be free to use and/or adapt the materials in any way they wished after completion of the evaluation. All teachers who participated in the study appeared to appreciate the need for uniform procedures, and were extremely co-operative in this respect.

Justification for selecting a target age-group of 12- to 13-year-olds was based on two main reasons. First, as described in Chapter 1, there is a considerable amount of evidence from surveys and other sources that by the ages of 12 and 13 the majority of British adolescents have some experience of drinking alcohol. Second, many educationalists whose experience contributed to this study felt that most school-based alcohol education begins too late, and they were strongly in favour of involving 12- to 13-year-olds in alcohol education.

Overall, the package was presented to teachers as having two principal aims:

(1) To provide a framework which will allow pupils to think about alcohol in a way which is relevant to their own immediate and perceived future experience.
(2) To help pupils begin to develop the necessary skills to make reasoned choices about alcohol.

(Bagnall 1990: 1)

The content of the package was subdivided into various activities, some for small group work and discussion, some for completion by individual pupils, and others for use with the class as a large group. These activities were reproduced on worksheets, a set of which was included in the Manual for Teachers. Where appropriate, correct answers were provided on the teacher's copy. Each pupil received his/her own personal set of worksheets.

Individual activities in the package

The alcohol education programme began with an activity which does not even mention alcohol! The first exercise was about choice and decision-making in a variety of everyday situations. It was intended to help adolescents realise that they are constantly having to make choices, and that their chosen option may include that of saying 'no'. The second part of this activity was intended to encourage recognition of the need for accurate information to help make reasoned choices.

The package then went on to provide such information on the topic of alcohol. Pupils participated in activities which aimed to increase knowledge about alcohol and its effects on their bodies and behaviour. This included an exercise on the relative strengths of different alcoholic drinks, an aspect of the package which several of the participating teachers admitted was new information for them also. Such information was intended to dispel popular myths about alcohol. These included the 'false' notion that cider has a much lower alcoholic content than beers, that all beers are the same strength, and that drinking spirits is much more harmful than drinking beers. The activities on the effects of alcohol included references to the risks of intoxication. These focused on situations relevant to the life-styles of 12- to 13-year-olds, including swimming and cycling. The positive effects of alcohol were also acknowledged – for example, its value as a 'social lubricant'. This follows the argument that teachers will more readily secure the confidence of their pupils in the objectivity of the alcohol programme if 'some attention is paid to enjoyment of responsible alcohol use' (Finn 1977: 18). It has already been noted that one of the objectives of the education package was to stress relevance of content to the target group. For this reason the issue of driving a vehicle under the influence of alcohol was not included; nor were long-term effects of heavy consumption such as liver cirrhosis discussed. Despite this, it must be remembered that the flexibility of small group discussion would allow any adolescent with personal experience of such issues to raise them in the group if desired.

At this point the educational emphasis of the package focused on the 'social influences' approach as discussed in Chapter 1. There it was noted that this approach aims to develop a critical awareness of social pressures encouraging young people to drink alcohol. In addition, there was some evidence that this approach may be an effective way to tackle the problem of educating young people about alcohol. In this package the particular social influences selected included peer group pressure, parental attitudes and media messages about alcohol. Peer group pressure and parental attitudes were examined by using fictitious case studies as a stimulus for small group discussion. Story completion was offered as an individual activity on these case studies and optional role-play recommended if the teacher felt confident that this would be productive with her/his particular class. These latter two methods were intended to allow the young people not just to develop a critical awareness, but to practice some resistance to social pressure in a fictitious and ideally non-threatening situation.

The activities examining the influence of the mass media were two-fold. The negative image of alcohol prevalent in newspaper headlines, especially the tabloids, was presented, along with the positive image from alcohol advertisements. These activities encouraged pupils to analyse the contrasting messages and the techniques of presentation (for example, the use of 'shock-horror' headlines in tabloids, or the association of alcohol in advertisements with fun, sex appeal, music, bright colours, sporting success and glamorous lifestyles). In addition, it was suggested that small group discussion be encouraged about the presentation of alcohol in television drama and soap-opera. The Manual for Teachers strongly recommended that these activities be extended beyond the classroom to the family home. In this way it was intended to provide an opportunity for parental involvement in the alcohol education programme.

The final activity in the package was a 'quiz', which could be completed individually, in teams, or as a class group. The function of this activity was mainly one of consolidation, helping pupils to recap and assess for themselves what they had learned from the package. (This quiz was also the main component of the measure of alcohol-related knowledge used in the questionnaire surveys.)

Some of these activities incorporated alcohol education materials already available (Teachers Advisory Council on Alcohol and Drug Education/Health Education Council 1984, and Scottish Health Education Group 1985) and the author is grateful for permission to include these. Wherever possible activities were illustrated, with cartoon-based humour playing a prominent role. Colour reproduction was utilised in the main evaluation study (not in the pilot) to provide stimulus material for the activity on alcohol advertising. Unfortunately this proved very costly, and it was only possible to provide one set of material of rather inferior quality for each class. This, of course, was not a problem in the published version of the teaching pack (Bagnall 1990).

In its final format, the package required about four hours of teaching time.

CHANGES RESULTING FROM PILOTING THE PACKAGE

Before the commencement of the main study, the educational materials had been tested in three large state comprehensive schools in Lothian region. One of these was situated in an area of severe social deprivation and one teacher there commented: 'If it goes down well here it will go down well anywhere!' In fact the package was well received by staff in this school, who felt it was filling a gap in their resources.

A second 'pilot school' was situated in a new town in the central lowland belt of Scotland, and here the alcohol education was not allocated a full guidance period each week as in the other two schools. Instead it was taught for a short period (twenty minutes) every morning in small 'tutor groups'. This, however, was reported to be problematic by all participating staff, who found that a longer session was required to complete individual activites to a satisfactory level.

The third 'pilot school' was largely 'middle-class'; once again the package was allocated to the weekly guidance period and was enthusiastically received.

Teachers participating in the piloting of the education materials completed detailed 'feedback forms' and were subsequently interviewed by the author. Short feedback forms were also collected from participating pupils. The principal recommendations from this piloting were:

(a) The package should be shortened (it had included two further activities in addition to those described above). One activity was removed because it proved complex for both teachers and pupils. The other was rejected because a majority of pupils found it patronising – 'It's like what we did in primary school' was a common criticism.
(b) Colour should be included, and in general the quality of the stimulus materials improved. School pupils and teachers are generally used to working with high quality printed resources, and there is no doubt that the pilot version of the alcohol education package was poorly reproduced. However, 'high-gloss' is expensive, and the compromise solution in the main study was to utilise professional expertise for all illustrations (in black and white) and use colour reproductions of alcohol advertisements.
(c) A small number of minor modifications to text and layout were required.

These recommendations were all incorporated into the version of the package used for the main evaluation study. Once again, feedback was obtained from teachers and pupils. This is discussed in the next chapter. However, it is worth noting here that, as in the piloting of the materials, teachers in the main study commented on the 'low-gloss' nature of the package. They were, however, prepared to accept that the main purpose of the research had been to conduct a scientific evaluation of one approach to alcohol education. It was to this end that resources had been invested, in terms of both time and finance.

Chapter 5

Comments from the classroom: what the teachers and pupils thought

THE SPECIALIST TEACHERS

In Chapter 2 it was noted that five teachers were seconded for a short period of time to work on the project, and in particular to assist with the development of the alcohol education package. These teachers were selected with the assistance of senior advisers in the education authority, and were chosen primarily for their experience, commitment and proven capabilities in the field of health/social education. In each region the teacher(s) recommended by the senior adviser were visited by the author to discuss their potential involvement in the project. Fortunately all teachers who had been recommended were willing to take on the role of 'specialist teacher' in their region, despite the additional workload that this would entail. As would be expected within the English, Welsh and Scottish education systems, none of the five teachers who participated in this way taught health/social education on a full-time basis, and all had teaching commitments in their own discipline. These subject areas were different for all of the five teachers, and covered humanities, modern languages, mathematics, chemistry and religious studies. There were three females and two males with a wide range of age and teaching experience.

At the end of stage two of the study, that is, the teaching of the alcohol education, each of these five teachers was asked to submit a written report of their experiences on the project. Extracts from these reports form the remainder of this section. Sadly, one report was never received as the teacher involved tragically died. Although his report cannot be included, I would like to take the opportunity here to acknowledge the effort, commitment and sense of humour which he contributed to this research study.

It will be remembered that the author had attempted to standardise the way in which the alcohol education package was taught, by requesting close adherence to the guidelines in the Manual for Teachers. In reality, however, it is clearly impossible to rule out completely the individual influence of any one teacher. Pupils' receptiveness to the alcohol education package will obviously be dependent to some extent on such 'teacher effect'. This is particularly true in terms of rapport between teacher and pupils, and of the teacher's confidence and skills in handling small group work. More generally, the teacher's personal competence in teaching material which places such a heavy emphasis on pupil participation must play an important role. Against this, however, as already detailed in Chapter 2, the 'specialist' teachers in this study were chosen precisely for their experience and skills in these areas. Such abilities are a basic attribute of all teachers actively involved in social education of any kind. Furthermore, the 'non-specialist' teachers who participated in this evaluation study all had some involvement in health and social education programmes in addition to teaching their own subject. By involving only teachers with this kind of experience, it was intended to minimise variation due to 'teacher effect'. Fortunately, this decision was reinforced by the statistical results of the study (see Chapter 6), and by the more anecdotal reports from teachers which are discussed in the remainder of this chapter.

Reports from 'specialist teachers'

Involvement of the 'seconded' teachers in the development of the package was seen by participants as a useful experience, and was summed up by one of them as follows:

> The meeting with teachers to produce the package showed that there was fairly close agreement that:
> - alcohol education needed to be tackled
> - the methods were similar to those used in other areas of the curriculum
> - a variety of approaches should be tried
> - teachers might eventually be able to choose from a range of material
>
> The [resulting] package was very acceptable to us in material content and methodology. In future we would incorporate some slide or film material to vary the style of presentation of information.

This last comment reflects one of the more controversial issues discussed amongst these teachers, with three of the five insisting strongly that the package should include a video or film as a trigger to group discussion. However, agreement was finally reached that this would not be included in the evaluation study for two main reasons:

(i) it would be too costly to produce within the budget of the project, and
(ii) not all schools could assume access to the necessary equipment at an appropriate point in the alcohol education programme.

The Manual for Teachers was found to be useful by these 'specialist' teachers, who appear to have experienced little difficulty in following the guidelines for teaching each activity in the package. One teacher reported: 'The Teacher's Manual was useful. I found it easy to teach the package. Although I found the worksheet on the effects of alcohol on the body was not easy to understand, the pupils had no problems'. And a second said:

> I generally found the groups worked well. I did not find the prescriptive approach of the Teacher's Manual unacceptable or frustrating. This was probably because of the novelty of the topic for our pupils. If they had regarded it as 'the same old stuff' more innovative teaching approaches might have been required to add interest.

A third teacher concluded: 'The material was easy to use and generally well received by pupils'.

As might be predicted, the issue of how the alcohol education package would be utilised in their schools after the research study was completed raised a variety of comments. Perceived future implementation of alcohol education depends very much on existing provision of timetable space, resources and facilities for such a 'minority' subject.

One teacher took the opportunity in her report to indicate some general as well as specific recommendations:

> Health Education should ideally be included in the Core Curriculum so that all pupils have the information which they require. There is no need to try to avoid duplication of topics e.g. by Biology and Social Education, since there can be variety in approach. In later years pupils should be directed towards the effect of alcohol abuse on relationships and attitudes. The pupil's

ability to solve problems should also be an approach to this topic. Alcohol Education should be treated separately from drug education – the use of alcohol is socially acceptable and so young people are expected to make acceptable decisions on the position they are going to take up when forced to make a choice. The longer-term effects of alcohol abuse may be included with drug abuse.

And, more specifically, she indicated that: 'In the school situation, we would present this as part of (a) an Alcohol Education programme presented cyclically over two or three years with presentations to suit each group, and (b) A Health Education programme'.

More negatively she added that 'We did not consider the package as part of a possible "whole school" programme'.

The format for such a programme was perceived more in terms of the topic of alcohol misuse being discussed in a specific context chosen for its appropriateness to a particular year group.

This teacher went on to recommend that:

Teachers involved in each school might be asked to decide on aspects, materials and methods to be used with each year group in the school. Consideration might be given to the allocation of the following topics to appropriate year groups:

Alcohol abuse and
- non-accidental injury of children
- single parents
- road accidents
- cost of treatment of alcohol victims
- cost of treatment of alcoholics
- related disease
- the GP
- the family
- employment

The timing of the alcohol educational intervention in the evaluation study was favoured. One teacher reported that 'We feel the timing was right because many of these pupils drink alcohol'. And a second participant in a different school concluded that 'The age group was ideal – the majority of our pupils of that age are interested in alcohol'. However, the latter teacher felt that continued use of the package in its entirety would require more formal allocation to alcohol education in the timetable – ideally to allow one social education period (forty minutes) per week for the duration of the package.

Perhaps all these ideas can best be summarised by the opening comment in one teacher's report: 'The package was very useful and enjoyable to teach. I will definitely use at least some of the materials in years to come'.

It could be argued, of course, that those teachers who provided reports, because of their close involvement in the development of the package were, not unnaturally, predisposed to be positive about it. However, they were also quite willing to make suggestions for improvements, based on their experience of using the materials with pupils.

One criticism which emerged unanimously from the 'specialist' teachers was shortage of time: 'I would have liked more time to develop and/or debrief group discussions' and 'more time would have facilitated build-up of rapport (between teacher and pupils)'.

A second source of criticism for all specialist teachers was the quality of the stimulus materials. As already noted, several of these teachers had argued strongly for inclusion of a film or video. Although this had not formed part of the alcohol education package eventually evaluated, the desire for future inclusion of such a resource was reinforced in the reports: 'In future we would incorporate some slide or film material to vary the style of presentation of information'. Two further teachers suggested that the fictitious case study used to stimulate discussion about parental attitudes and peer group pressure 'needs a video as an added stimulus. On its own the story is too short and the outcomes too obvious'.

THE 'NON-SPECIALIST' TEACHERS

In addition to the detailed written reports from the 'specialist' teachers, feedback was also obtained from the teachers in the project who had been asked to teach the alcohol education package without any prior involvement in its development. Included with each copy of the Manual for Teachers was a short 'Feedback Form for Teachers', to be filled in and returned to the Alcohol Research Group on completion of the teaching package. The questions in the form were intended to provide information on these teachers' reactions to their initial experience of the package. Specific information was sought on agreement or otherwise with the overall rationale of the alcohol education, with the objectives for individual pupil activities and with the appropriateness of the content for the target group. Comments were also invited on the teaching methods used in the package, with the opportunity to highlight any component of the materials which they did not like having to teach, and any difficulties experienced. A final open-ended question invited general comments on this experience of teaching the alcohol education package. At the beginning of the form teachers were reminded that it was completely anonymous, and they were consequently urged to be absolutely honest in all their comments. In addition it was made clear that constructive criticism would be welcomed, as it formed an important component of the evaluation study. In their everyday professional lives, few teachers have the opportunity to influence the fundamental content of their curriculum. It was therefore hoped that they would appreciate and take advantage of this opportunity to participate actively in the formulation of new curriculum materials, indicating modifications which they personally believed to be necessary.

Feedback forms were returned by eighteen teachers, covering a wide range of age, academic discipline and experience of teaching. Of course, all these staff had in common the fact that they were currently involved in teaching health/social education, this being the principal reason for their inclusion in the study. However, even at this level, there was a wide range of experience, from principal teacher of social education with over ten years' of experience, to a 'newcomer' with only two month's experience in this area of teaching.

Some of the more critical comments resulting from these forms included:

'Any final production [of the package] would no doubt have a professional layout and colour. The pupils in the main found the lack of colour and the layout uninspiring'.
'They really need a film or video starter stimulus'.
'The adverts needed to be *poster* size, and the pupils could have done poster work to go with this exercise'.
'We [this is assumed to refer to teacher and pupils] tended to feel there was a lack of variety'.
'All in all I felt the material wasn't "teacher proof". We delivered it as instructed, but without input of our own (which we restrained ourselves from doing) it was a bit arid'.

More generally there was unanimous agreement with the overall rationale of the package, and only three out of the eighteen staff felt that any of the defined objectives for individual activities in the package were unrealistic. The use of small group work was popular, with only one teacher experiencing any great difficulty in maintaining group discussion.

Responses to the final open-ended question were very encouraging, with the majority expressing a positive reaction to the approach of the package, and to its limited content. Most who responded here said they would continue to make use of the materials and several mirrored the comment: 'I look forward to any new, glossy version'. Only one teacher expressed reservations about future use; she felt that the materials had been problematic for less able pupils, and were in any case more relevant to older pupils. The two most frequent recommendations were for:

(a) additional visual aids, especially for the activity on alcohol advertising;
(b) additional information about the effects of alcohol, perhaps including a video.

Most teachers expressed the need for more time and flexibility in presentation of the package.

Pupil feedback

Pupils who participated in the study were also asked to complete a 'feedback sheet' at the end of the alcohol education package. As with the teachers, these sheets were completed anonymously. Once again, this confidentiality was strongly reinforced in order to urge the young people to be honest in their comments. Although it was subsequently possible for teachers to look through the completed forms from their classes, there was no indication of pupil identity. In fact teachers were interested to read these forms before posting them off to the Alcohol Research Group. As several of the staff noted, pupils very seldom have an opportunity to comment formally on curriculum matters, especially to 'outsiders'. Perhaps because of this the teachers felt that the forms had been completed quite honestly. As would be expected, however, some of the young people had not taken the exercise seriously, and filled in meaningless (but sometimes amusing) answers.

The pupils were asked which activity in the alcohol education package they liked most, and which they liked least. In each case they were asked to explain their answer. They were then asked if they had learned anything from the package that they did not already know, and if so, what. Finally, as in the feedback form for teachers, there was an open-ended question inviting pupils to make any other comments about the package.

For a variety of reasons the pupil feedback data have not been analysed in any quantitative sense. The nature of the data collection was very crude, and there is no way of guaranteeing that pupils felt completely uninhibited when completing the forms, depending on the nature of teacher supervision at the time. There is also clear evidence from the forms that several youngsters copied each other's answers. Furthermore, there is no guarantee that staff (at any level in the school hierarchy) did not select those forms which were posted to the Alcohol Research Group, perhaps removing any which were excessively rude or negative. Such forms could have been perceived as reflecting badly on the school or on a particular teacher.

Forms were received from over 500 pupils, out of a possible 1,055 respondents. The main explanation for the missing data is that two schools involved in teaching the alcohol education package failed to return the forms for their pupils. This obviously introduces a potential bias into the data that were received. Missing reports from schools which did return the forms can be explained by pupil absenteeism, and by the fact that not all teachers in each school completed this final exercise with their class.

Despite these methodological problems, the pupil data does give some general but useful qualitative insight into how the package was perceived by the young people for whom it was developed.

Predictably, there was a full range of responses to the questions concerning popularity of individual activities in the education package. Activities which were rated as most popular with some pupils were also rated as least popular with others. For instance, many pupils rated the introductory activity on making choices as 'the best' for reasons such as: 'It was easy to understand', 'It was fun to do', and 'Because it was things to do with us'. Conversely, a similar proportion of pupils rated this activity as the one they liked least. The reasons given for this included: 'Because it was quite boring', 'Some of the choices were hard', 'Because it doesn't tell a lot', and 'Because it was difficult to think in the way that we had to'.

The reasons given to justify choice of activity as most or least liked were generally uninformative, with 'it was boring' the most frequently quoted reason for not liking an activity. Obviously, the way in which any activity is rated by an individual pupil will depend on a variety of factors, including personal interests, background knowledge and experience, and the way in which the activity is presented by the class teacher. (It will be remembered from Chapter 4 that this was one of the reasons why the alcohol education package had been based on an educational application of Kelly's personal construct theory, and so emphasised pupil participation.)

Given these difficulties, it is interesting to observe that there was a clear indication that the two most 'factual' activities were rated as most popular across all schools who returned forms. These exercises concerned the equivalent alcoholic strengths of different drinks and the effects of alcohol both on the body and on behaviour. Reasons given for choosing the first of these as the activity liked most included:

'Because it was helpful and interesting'
'Because it shows how much alcohol really was in the drink'
'Because it told the readers something about quantities of drinks'

These observations were reinforced in the responses to the question asking pupils what, if anything, they had learned from the alcohol education package. The same two 'factual' activities featured repeatedly here with the exercise on equivalent alcoholic strengths being the most frequently quoted. Some examples of these responses are reproduced below:

[Can you note down something you have learned?]

'I learn't the measures of alcohol'
'How much wine and how much beer etc.'
'About some of the units of alcohol'
'The amounts of alcohol compared in different alcohol drinks, and what can happen to you'
'I didn't know that some small drinks are worse than some large drinks'
'Alcohol harms you as much as drugs'
'I have learned what drink can do to you'
'that eating with drink slows down the effect'
'that it (alcohol) is more dangerous to a woman than to a man'
'Alcohol is dangerous for bad health and a lot is bad for your body'

Finally, a selection of responses to the open-ended question asking for general comments on the package is quoted below. Many pupils omitted this question, but once again a wide range of responses occurred amongst those who answered. Some of these were unprintable, and some were quite negative:

'It was OK but boring'
'It was boring and pointless as no-one learnt hardly anthing'
'It could of been better – too much writing'
'It was a bit long and would have been more interesting to have more drama'
'It was something to do during our Social Education lesson'

However, such comments were outweighed by a more positive reaction from the majority of respondents, as indicated below:

'It was interesting and fun to do'
'It will be useful when I get older'
'It made us think more about alcohol and how it effects us'
'It was a good exercise and put over messages good'
'Most of it was very interesting'

Implications of comments from teachers and pupils

As already noted above, many of the comments from pupils were idiosyncratic, with several activities in the alcohol education package liked and disliked by similar proportions of pupils. However, two activities which were observed to elicit a consistently positive response were those giving factual information about alcohol. This could indicate a potential problem for the alcohol education package. It may be remembered from Chapter 2 that there is some evidence to suggest that substance misuse education which only gives factual information has been shown to encourage experimentation with the psychoactive substance in question. Could this then suggest potential risk for young people in the alcohol education study who rated the factual activities most highly? To consider this possibility it is necessary to exercise caution in interpreting the qualitative data obtained in the present study. First, the 'crudeness' of the data has already been acknowledged above. Furthermore, it may be that the more factual activities were referred to by more pupils simply because of the more tangible nature of their content. Open-ended and more abstract activities make less conscious impact and are less likely to be recalled. Certainly there is little doubt that activities concerned with the development of skills and awareness of social influences have a much less concrete outcome, especially in the short term. The quantitative analysis discussed in Chapter 6 includes an examination of how these young people's alcohol-related attitudes and behaviour changed, as well as their factual knowledge about the substance. As will be seen there, there is some indication that the alcohol education did have some influence beyond merely improving knowledge.

The qualitative information from teachers suggests that the programme successfully achieved its major objectives of providing teachers with an inexpensive, easy-to-use alcohol education package, demanding little preparation time or in-service training. In general the package appeared to be welcomed in its existing structure, and most of the specific comments from teachers were encouraging. The most common criticisms concerned the poor quality of the resource materials in the education package, and a lack of time to develop group work adequately. The participating teachers were very tolerant of the constraints imposed on their use of the package for the purposes of the research methodology. It is hoped that any problems related to these constraints will be overcome when the package is used in a non-experimental setting. Under such conditions teachers will be free to use the alcohol education materials as they wish, adjusting the content and timing to suit their specific timetable, and to meet the educational needs of any particular class or group of young people. Such flexibility should also overcome some of the expressed difficulty with less able pupils, where the pace and presentation of the materials can be modified appropriately.

It is to be hoped that the alcohol education package can fit comfortably into an existing health education curriculum without excessive modification. However, it must also be remembered that the package developed for the research study was self-contained, and evaluated as such. It follows that the findings from this evaluation may not hold for any subsequent versions of the package which have been subjected to a large amount of alteration, such as reordering or ommission of activities.

Problems concerning the quality of the stimulus materials were evident in the comments from participating teachers. As noted in Chapter 4, this has been rectified with professional publication of the alcohol education package (Bagnall 1990). Due to commercial sponsorship the cost of this improved version of the alcohol education package has been kept to a minimum, despite the use of colour and high quality materials.

Teachers who subsequently purchase the package for use in their schools will of course be free to supplement the resource in any way they choose, for example, by the inclusion of an appropriate video.

In this way the qualitative findings from the evaluation study have played an important formative role in the resulting alcohol education package for teachers.

Chapter 6

Was the alcohol education effective?

In Chapter 2 there is a description of how the research was carried out in this study. This was described as a three-stage process:

(a) Baseline survey of alcohol-related knowledge, attitudes and behaviour.
(b) Development and administration of the alcohol education package.
(c) Follow-up survey of alcohol-related knowledge, attitudes and behaviour.

So far the first two parts of this process have been described in detail. Chapter 3 concentrated on the baseline survey, in order to give a picture of how the adolescents in the study used and misused alcohol prior to the educational intervention. The picture which emerged was one of a group of young people who almost all have some experience of alcohol. This experience, however, was extremely limited for the majority, with only a small proportion reporting that they had drunk alcohol in large quantities. Furthermore, very few of the study group reported regular consumption of alcohol, with very occasional intoxication being the most commonly reported form of misuse. It was noted that these findings are reinforced by several other surveys of young people and alcohol. These other surveys also suggest that the amounts of alcohol young people consume, and the frequency with which they consume it, are likely to increase as they progress through adolescence. On the basis of evidence such as this, there is a strong case for targeting alcohol education at 12- to 13-year-olds. At this age most of them have at least tasted an alcoholic drink, and so the education is not introducing a topic about which they have no relevant experience. On the other hand, only a small minority of these young people have experienced noteworthy problems as a result of their alcohol consumption. So it can be argued that alcohol education is highly appropriate at this age, intervening in a behaviour which has already been initiated, but which has not as yet caused any widespread problems.

Adopting these arguments, the alcohol education package for this study was developed to integrate content and educational method appropriate to a target group of 12- to 13-year-olds. The educational rationale underlying the resulting package was discussed in Chapter 4, along with some specific examples of its content. Details were also provided of how the alcohol education was administered in the participating schools. Chapter 5 focused on the reaction of teachers and pupils to the alcohol education and a generally favourable response was noted.

With phases one and two of the project thus described, only the final stage, the follow-up survey, remains for detailed discussion. This is in many respects the most crucial aspect of the entire study and will form the remainder of the present chapter.

As illustrated in Figure 2.2 of Chapter 2, the study group was subdivided for the second phase of the project, the alcohol education, into three groups. The first group, t_1 in Figure 2.3, had the four-hour alcohol education programme taught by their 'everyday' social/health education teachers. These teachers had no special training before teaching the alcohol materials. The second experimental group, t_2 in Figure 2.2, had the alcohol education taught to them by the 'specialist' teachers who had been actively involved in the development of the material. The third subgroup in the study, the control group (C), had no exposure to the alcohol education package. All three groups, t_1, t_2 and C, completed the baseline survey at the beginning of the project and, approximately eighteen months later, the follow-up survey.

As noted above, other surveys of young people and alcohol would suggest that the 12- to 13-year-olds in the present study would exhibit some change in their alcohol-related knowledge, attitudes and behaviour between the two surveys merely as a result of growing older. In particular, an increase in their experience of alcohol would be expected. However, if the alcohol educational intervention had any measurable effect, there should be differences between the adolescents who received the education, and those in the study who had no alcohol education. The study had been designed to facilitate examination of any such differences and to relate these to the administration of the alcohol education programme. It is in this way that the effectiveness of the alcohol education could be judged.

DIFFERENCES ARISING BETWEEN BASELINE AND FOLLOW-UP SURVEYS

Experience of alcohol – total study group

As expected, the follow-up survey showed that all the young people in the study group reported an increase in their experience of alcohol and its effects. They were becoming older, and such changes are consistent with the findings from other studies (Plant, *et al.* 1985; Marsh, *et al.* 1986). These changes included quantity of alcohol consumed on last occasion, experience of hangover and other examples which are illustrated in Table 6.1.

Table 6.1 Experience of alcohol – before and after the educational intervention

Survey question	Percentage of study group who responded 'Yes'	
	Pre-intervention survey	Post-intervention survey
Ever tasted an alcoholic drink	96	98
Drunk alcohol in last seven days	15	23
Ever had a hangover	20	33
> 4 hangovers in last 6 months	1	4
Alcohol-induced stomach upset	27	29
Alcohol-related accident/injury	4	6
Maximum consumption of ⩾ 8 units of alcohol (4 pints of beer)	9	22

But the fundamental issue which had to be addressed concerned differences between the intervention and control groups. Although the study group as a whole exhibited an increase in self-reported experience of alcohol, was this increase larger for the control group schools who received no alcohol education? In other words, had exposure to the alcohol education programme had any moderating effect on subsequent alcohol use? Second, had the alcohol education contributed to any improvements in knowledge about alcohol amongst the two intervention groups? And third, did the control and intervention groups differ in their attitudes about alcohol?

In order to answer these questions, a fairly complex statistical model was adopted. For readers with an interest in these matters the model is explained in Appendix 2. However, the following discussion is intended to be comprehended without the need to understand the statistical analyses in any depth. The only assumption underlying what follows is a minimal understanding of the concept of probability levels, as described in Chapter 3. Differences between control and intervention groups were examined, not only for the study group as a whole, but also for males and females separately. Few gender differences emerged, and in the discussion which follows, the findings for males and females independently will only be quoted where they did differ significantly.

Alcohol-related knowledge

The first of the three questions to be considered concerns alcohol-related knowledge. As may be recalled from Chapter 3, respondents' knowledge about alcohol was assessed by a 'quiz' of fifteen items, asking about such 'facts' as the equivalent strengths of different alcoholic drinks. The average score for knowledge items correct out of fifteen was calculated for each school in the study. This figure increased for all schools, between baseline and follow-up surveys, and is illustrated for each experimental group in Table 6.2.

Table 6.2 Average scores on knowledge quiz (maximum score 15) – before and after the alcohol education

Group	Average score (correct) Before	Average score (correct) After	Change in average score
t_1 (non-specialist teachers)	6.7	8.3	+1.6
t_2 (specialist teachers)	6.1	7.9	+1.8
C (control group)	6.4	7.4	+1.0

From Table 6.2 it is clear that the young people in the two groups receiving the alcohol education showed a slightly better improvement than those in the comparison group. This suggests that the alcohol education, which contained factual information relevant to the quiz, may have contributed to the subsequent alcohol-related knowledge of the intervention groups. Despite this difference, however, it is obvious that the real increase in knowledge was very small for all sub-groups. For this and other reasons which will become apparent, the differences in knowledge between the groups were not statistically significant. The conclusion has to be drawn that the average score correct on the knowledge quiz was not significantly influenced by exposure to the alcohol education package.

Respondents' knowledge about alcohol was further examined. In particular, comparisons were made on correct answers for individual items in the knowledge quiz. For thirteen out of the fifteen individual items, there were no statistically significant differences between the subgroups in the study. At this stage, however, there were two items where the young people who had been educated about alcohol were significantly more likely than the comparison group to answer correctly. These items were:

(i) 'A single whisky (pub measure) is stronger than one pint of beer', and
(ii) 'Alcohol harms more people in Britain than illegal drugs such as heroin or cocaine'.

Results were already beginning to look a little more encouraging. However, there were also emerging suspicions that some of the data may somehow have been 'contaminated' and these were gradually reinforced. For one of the schools which had not received the alcohol education, the responses on separate knowledge items were consistently better than those for the other schools in the control group. This apparent anomaly was investigated by making appropriate enquiries, which led to the conclusion that the data had indeed been subject to local contamination. Although not exposed to the alcohol education package in the present study, the 12- to 13-year-olds in this particular control group school had been actively involved in an alternative alcohol education programme. During the period between the baseline and follow-up survey this school should have received no alcohol education of any kind. Unfortunately, however, it had participated in a separate health education initiative, which was held concurrently and involved young people in schools and community organisations throughout Wales. Factual information about tobacco and alcohol misuse played an important part in this programme. It looked as though participation in this Welsh programme could have been responsible for an improvement in alcohol-related knowledge not found in the other control group schools. While this may be encouraging for the Welsh programme, it was an unfortunate development for the alcohol education study under discussion here. However, it also has to be viewed as one of the potential problems of fieldwork in the social sciences. Scientific purity may be the idealistic goal in this kind of research, but the real world of human beings seldom conforms to the requirements of such idealism. It is reasonably straightforward to set up a controlled study in the physics or chemistry laboratory. Once outside such a setting, however, it becomes much more difficult, and sometimes impossible, to eliminate external influences which may affect the subject matter under investigation.

Because of the apparent contamination of control group data, it was decided to reanalyse the results for individual knowledge items. This time the analysis would exclude the 'contaminated' control group school and the two other schools in that region. When restricted to two regions in this way, the reanalysis highlighted several additional aspects of alcohol-related knowledge which appeared to have been enhanced by the educational intervention. These items are shown in Table 6.3, where significant differences between control and intervention groups are noted. In addition, the comparison was subdivided to look for further differences between males and females. Some studies evaluating health education have found that knowledge improvement is more likely to result amongst females. However, as Table 6.3 shows, this was not apparent in the present findings.

Table 6.3 Knowledge items influenced by intervention*

Quiz item	Males and females	Males only	Females only
'A single whisky (as measured in a pub) is stronger than one pint of beer'.	NS	NS	$p<0.1$
'Eating along with drinking will slow down the effects of alcohol'.	NS	NS	$p<0.1$
'Alcohol harms less people in Britain than illegal drugs such as heroin or cocaine'.	$p<0.1$	$p<0.01$	NS
'The human body gets rid of two pints of beer in one hour'.	NS	$p<0.05$	NS
'It can be dangerous to drink alcohol if you have taken tablets or medicine'.	$p<0.05$	$p<0.05$	$p<0.05$

Notes: NS = not significant
* 'contaminated' data omitted

Although there were some aspects of alcohol-related knowledge where only females improved noticeably, there were others where only males appeared to have been receptive to this aspect of the education package. Overall, males and females did not differ in how much they had learned about alcohol as a result of the intervention.

In conclusion then, the impact of the alcohol education on the alcohol-related knowledge of the 12- to 13-year-olds in the study was somewhat greater than had initially been apparent, although overall there was still scope for considerable improvement.

Alcohol-related attitudes

The attitudes of the study group towards alcohol use were measured using a set of twenty short statements about alcohol, reflecting a mixture of favourable and unfavourable attitudes. Respondents were asked to tick whether they agreed, disagreed or were not sure about each of these statements. The way in which this information was integrated into positive and negative attitude 'scores' respectively has been described in Chapter 3. Approval of alcohol consumption was taken to imply a positive attitude, while disapproval was taken to imply a negative attitude towards its use.

Table 6.4 illustrates the findings for alcohol-related attitudes, broken down by experimental group.

Table 6.4 Attitude change by group

	Control group (C)		Intervention group 1 (t_2)		Intervention group 2 (t_1)	
	Positive attitudes	Negative attitudes	Positive attitudes	Negative attitudes	Positive attitudes	Negative attitudes
% Increase	59.2	30.8	63.5	34.3	59.8	43.4
% Decrease	26.1	57.1	25.5	56.4	26.8	46.8
% Same	14.7	12.0	11.0	9.3	13.4	9.8

The percentage increase refers to respondents whose score on the respective attitude scales increased between the two surveys. In other words, the figures describe respectively the proportion of respondents in each group who became more positive about alcohol use and the proportion who became less positive.

From Table 6.4 it can be seen that approximately 60 per cent of respondents in all three experimental groups exhibited an increase in positive attitudes. There was little difference between those who did and those who did not receive the alcohol education. This suggests that the educational intervention had no influence on the recognised tendency for adolescents to develop more positive attitudes to alcohol as they grow older. It might have been expected that the alcohol education would result in a less positive attitude to alcohol use, as demonstrated by lowering of the score on the positive attitudes scale. This, however, was not supported. On the other hand, there was an indication that, although not significantly different from the rest, more of the 'educated' youngsters had become more negative about alcohol as implied by total score on the attitude scales. This may have occured simply because the latter were more likely than the control group youngsters to choose the 'not sure' option when completing the attitude scales. However, it may also be that the alcohol education had encouraged some of its recipients to be a little more negative towards alcohol consumption. There was no obvious contamination effect on the raw data for alcohol-related attitudes. This was confirmed by a reanalysis of the data excluding the three Welsh schools. The outcome was very similar to that for the complete study group. It thus appeared that attitudes to alcohol as measured in the present study were unaffected by the alternative health education campaign in Wales.

One can really only speculate on the issues discussed in this section on attitudes, and overall it has to be concluded that the education had no significant impact on the alcohol-related attitudes of the study group.

Alcohol-related behaviour

Information about the behaviour of respondents in relation to alcohol had been elicited by a variety of questions. These focused on issues such as respondents' experience of the effects of alcohol (hangovers, upset stomachs, and so on), how often respondents consumed alcohol and how much was drunk.

The principal measures of alcohol-related behaviour used in this study are shown in Table 6.5. As with the data on knowledge and attitudes described above, the behaviour data in Table 6.5 is broken down into subgroups to help identify differences between intervention and control groups.

Table 6.5 illustrates a consistent trend for the control group to have a higher response than the intervention groups. This is taken as an indication of greater experience of alcohol and its effects amongst the respondents who did not receive the education than amongst the respondents who did. For statistical reasons it is not always possible

Table 6.5 Alcohol-related behaviour changes following the educational intervention

Behavioural measures	Percentage C	t_2	t_1	Significance tests
(a) Ever had a hangover	20.8	18.1	14.8	NS
(b) Alcohol-induced stomach upset	16.1	13.7	13.4	NS
(c) Maximum consumption of > 3 units alcohol	45.6	36.8	38.9	$p<0.1$
(d) Alcohol consumed within last 7 days	31.3	20.7	24.6	$p<0.05$
(e) Increased frequency of consumption	56.0	50.4	53.4	NS

Notes: For (a) and (b) the percentages refer to respondents who answered 'No' at pre-test and 'Yes' at post-test.

For (c) and (d) the percentages refer to respondents who answered 'Yes' at post-test.

For (e) the percentages refer to respondents who indicated a higher frequency at post-test than at pre-test.

NS = not significant

to attribute the differences between the subgroups directly to the educational intervention. On the other hand, pupils who did not receive the alcohol education were significantly more likely to have drunk alcohol in the seven days prior to the follow-up survey. In addition, they were significantly more likely to have drunk more than three units of alcohol (that is, more than three glasses of wine or its equivalent) in one session. Generally then, the findings in Table 6.5 suggest that the alcohol education had some beneficial influence on the use of alcohol by those adolescents who were exposed to it.

As with the findings for alcohol-related attitudes, reanalysis excluding all the Welsh schools did not alter the pattern of results. This suggests that the 'behaviour' data had not been affected by the unforeseen exposure of the control group school to the alternative health initiative. This appears only to have influenced the measures of alcohol-related knowledge used in the present study.

CONCLUSION

The findings, discussed above, all suggest that the educational intervention in this study had a positive impact on the target group of 12-

to 13-year-olds. There is evidence that teenagers who were exposed to the package were more likely to know about the relative strengths of different alcoholic drinks; the impact of this was reinforced by pupils' own perceptions of what they had learned, as discussed in Chapter 5. With the contaminated data excluded, further 'improvement' in knowledge about alcohol can be attributed to the education programme.

It might have been predicted that exposure to alcohol education would limit the development of positive attitudes to alcohol. The results did not support this.

On the other hand, there was support for the expected increase in alcohol consumption and its associated consequences in the months between the two waves of data collection. Furthermore, the control group youngsters were more likely than others to demonstrate an increase in these behaviours. In particular, a significantly higher percentage of the control group had drunk alcohol in the previous week, and reported a higher maximum consumption.

In some controlled evaluation studies of health education, males and females have been found to differ in their responsiveness to the educational intervention (Gillies 1986; Hansen, *et al.* 1988). No significant gender differences, however, emerged in the present study. In addition, there was no evidence that the intervention was less effective when administered by teachers who had been given only a brief introduction prior to teaching the package.

It must be remembered that the package in this study was very short, requiring only four hours of classroom teaching time. It may be that a longer and more intensive intervention would have resulted in different degrees of responsiveness between males and females. A longer package may also have produced significant differences between the two intervention groups. The 'specialist' teachers, with the advantage of a simulated in-service training component, may have achieved a more positive impact.

Nevertheless, the findings discussed in this chapter do suggest that the alcohol education package specially developed for this study had a tangible and positive impact on the study group. Some improvement in knowledge about alcohol can be attributed to the package, although its influence on attitudes was less clear cut. Exposure to the package also appeared to have exerted some modest restraint on levels of alcohol consumption.

Furthermore, the qualitative findings from teacher and pupil reports indicated that the educational programme had achieved its major objectives of providing the educational community with an inexpensive and 'user-friendly' alcohol education package, demanding little in terms of preparation time or in-service training. Overall, the package appeared to be popular and useful, and was not obviously counterproductive.

Chapter 1 examined some of the rather depressing evidence on the effectiveness of education about alcohol and other drugs for young people. In the light of this, the findings from the present study, while not dramatic, are certainly encouraging. Chapter 1 also identified the low priority given to health education, let alone alcohol education, in the school curriculum. It has to be accepted that headteachers and school administrators are seldom willing to allocate much time in their curriculum to alcohol education. For these reasons, the education programme developed for this study was deliberately designed to be a minimal intervention. As a result of this it is unrealistic to expect large changes in the knowledge, attitudes and behaviour of young people as a direct consequence of four hours teaching spread over a period of weeks. It is therefore encouraging to be able to draw the conclusion that, unlike some previous drug and alcohol education programmes, this package had a modest but beneficial impact on the selected target group.

In Chapter 1 it was also noted that a longitudinal study of 1,036 school children in the Lothian region of Scotland had acted as a stimulus to the present project (Plant, *et al.* 1985). In the earlier study these authors had asked their 15- and 16-year-old respondents about alcohol education. Approximately 50 per cent of the study group recalled having received some alcohol education and amongst these there was an indication that: 'receiving alcohol education or seeing an alcohol education film are likely to be associated with higher levels of subsequent alcohol consumption and alcohol-related consequences, as well as with illicit drug experience' (Plant, *et al.* 1985: 101).

Reflecting on this puzzling association, the authors argued that:

> at face value those who had received alcohol education or who had seen alcohol education films became heavier users and misusers of alcohol and illicit drugs than did those who had not. It is, of course, possible that substance-oriented young people might be more likely to recall health education than those for whom alcohol and illicit drugs were less salient.
>
> (Plant, *et al.* 1985: 105)

Such results clearly lead one to question the value of any attempt to evaluate initiatives designed to educate young people about alcohol. However, as the authors themselves noted, their surveys did not ask for any detail about the extent or nature of the alcohol education recalled by these young people.

The important point emerging from studies like these is the need for careful and precise evaluation of specific approaches to alcohol education. As became evident in Chapter 1, the available evidence is controversial, with some interventions apparently having no effect, some having an effect opposite to the one intended, and some having the desired effect.

The present evaluation study has suggested that the approach to alcohol education used here falls into the latter category. This reinforces other studies which suggest that the way forward for educating young people about alcohol may well lie in an approach which emphasises potent social influences as well as individual skills and substance-based information.

Chapter 7

Conclusions and implications

The research project described in the preceding chapters had two sets of aims. The first of these was to conduct a systematic evaluation of the effectiveness of one approach to educating young people about alcohol. The evaluation was designed and carried out in a way which made it possible to quantify the effectiveness of the approach to alcohol education used in the study.

The second aim was to provide the teaching profession with an alcohol education package which was inexpensive and user-friendly, and which required minimal time for preparation and administration. An earlier pilot study had indicated that unless these conditions were met, the alcohol education package would be of little practical value. These conditions clearly imposed severe restrictions on the content and method of the alcohol education package. Nevertheless, as noted in Chapter 4, the perceived needs of the potential consumers were regarded as an important consideration in developing the teaching materials.

The opening chapters of this book have set the present alcohol education research in the wider context of health education. Some models of health-related behaviour were described, with the intention of highlighting the variety and complexity of reasons why young people may drink alcohol. This discussion was augmented by a brief review of the literature on the effectiveness of educating young people about alcohol and other drugs. Consideration was given to some of the difficulties of conducting this kind of research. These ranged from practical issues such as the validity and reliability of information obtained by questionnaire surveys about drinking, to the underlying assumptions and political implications of specific approaches to health education. The conclusions drawn from the literature on the effectiveness of health education were generally pessimistic. However, they also highlighted the importance of adopting a rigorous evaluation methodology, in order to establish what kind of approach really can be effective. Other points which emerged from the theoretical discussions had important implications for developing an alcohol education package for young people. First, the target group must be clearly defined, and the objectives of the planned educational intervention carefully formulated in relation to the chosen target groups. These objectives must be realistic, with open acknowledgement of any apparent limitations. If the objectives are overambitious and unrealistic, the likelihood of their being achieved is obviously reduced. It also became clear that the content of any alcohol educational initiative should emphasise relevance to the current life-styles and health-related behaviours of the chosen target group. Furthermore, there is some evidence that merely providing information about alcohol would be unlikely on its own to have the desired impact on the consumption behaviour of young people. A more positive outcome would be predicted by incorporating this information into an approach to alcohol education which helps young people to develop a critical awareness of some of the external pressures on their alcohol-related behaviour. The theoretical basis for this was discussed with particular reference to the 'social influences' approach to educating young people about alcohol, tobacco and illicit drugs.

Chapter 3 discussed the findings from the baseline survey, that is, the questionnaire filled in by all 12- to 13-year-olds in the study group before any of them were exposed to the alcohol education. This gave a detailed picture of the selected target group and alcohol, with information on how much they knew about alcohol, their attitudes towards it, and how they already used and misused it. Overall, the majority of young people in the study group had experienced few problems with alcohol. Nevertheless, a small proportion, more likely to be males, did report having had hangovers or alcohol-related stomach upsets. Comparisons with national and international data reinforced the general pattern that few 12- to 13-year-olds drink alcohol often, and when they do the amounts consumed are small. Longitudinal studies suggest that occasional adventures with alcohol and intoxication become more frequent as adolescence progresses and as drinking moves out of the family setting into licensed premises and discos, with peers rather than parents as companions. This, however, is not seen as an argument for postponing alcohol education beyond the age group of 12 to 13 years. Indeed, there may even be an argument for introducing alcohol education to younger children. A developmental study in Scotland showed that by age 6, children were already aware of alcohol, and could identify an alcoholic drink by smell. At the age of 8, youngsters held very negative attitudes about their own future use of alcohol, although the 12-year-olds in the study were much more positive (Jahoda and Cramond 1972). This suggests that children begin to develop their attitudes and beliefs about alcohol and its use well in advance of any real personal experience of the substance.

As the data in the baseline survey in the present study indicated, the majority of 12- to 13-year-olds had at least tried drinking alcohol; in other words, it is a substance of which they already have some personal experience. Furthermore, as these young people enter adolescence, they are beginning to develop some of the social skills associated with adulthood. In the context of alcohol these would include the self-confidence to question media messages and the ability to resist peer group pressure. The target group selected for this study would therefore seem an appropriate age at which to begin the process of developing responsible use of alcohol.

In Chapter 4, the development, piloting and implementation of the teaching package was described. It was noted that one of the strengths of this study was the contribution made by the experienced social/health education teachers who were co-opted to the project to assist with package development. In this way the research perspective was combined with the practical 'experiential' perspective of teachers themselves. The project thus benefited from knowledge and experience of educational research, from a review of the available literature on evaluating the effectiveness of alcohol education, and from the knowledge and classroom experience of teachers of social/health education.

The need to assess the education package had imposed severe limitations on the way in which it was implemented. As noted in Chapter 4, this was particularly evident in the request made to teachers to adhere closely to the guidelines for administering the alcohol education which were provided in the Manual for Teachers. This constraint was essential to minimise 'teacher effect' on the outcome of the study. However, it was also an unrealistic approach to teaching which did not reflect normal classroom practice, especially in social/health education. Constraints such as this gave participating schools little choice in how the alcohol education was administered to their classes of 12- to 13-year-olds. However, the implications for staffing are an important aspect of implementation which have to be considered when individual schools purchase the alcohol education teaching pack for their own private use. In Chapter 5 the comments from teachers involved in the research indicated that they had experienced no difficulty in following the administrative guidelines in the Manual for Teachers, which is an integral part of the pack. Although the package evaluated was devised as a free-standing module with a continuous theme, the objectives and suggested guidelines for teaching individual activities were self-contained. There should therefore be no difficulty for teachers who wish to select activities from the package without completing it in its entirety.

Chapters 5 and 6 focused on the results of the study, and attempted to answer the fundamental questions –

What did the teachers think of the alcohol education?
What did the pupils think?
What was the impact of this approach to alcohol education?

In Chapter 5 the qualitative findings from teachers and pupils were generally positive. Teachers, in particular, appeared very much in favour of the package, and many of them thought it filled an important gap in the curriculum. Several teachers indicated that they would continue to use the package after the end of the research investigation. On the negative side, both teachers and pupils were critical of the poor visual quality of the resource material in the package evaluated. There was also a demand for greater flexibility and for the optional inclusion of video as additional stimulus material. Most of these criticisms should be overcome by professional publication of the Teachers' Pack.

The qualitative data from pupils also indicated a generally favourable reaction to the alcohol education. Despite the weakness of this type of qualitative information, it is interesting to note that there was some parallel between the pupils' responses on their Feedback Forms, and their responses in the survey questionnaire. For instance, in the former, pupils were asked to write down anything they thought they had learned from the alcohol education package. A large proportion responded by referring to the equivalent strengths of different alcoholic drinks, suggesting this was an area of interest to them. In the quantitative data from the questionnaire survey, this was one of the aspects of alcohol-related knowledge which was assimilated by the young people who were exposed to the alcohol education.

The discussion in Chapter 6 addresses the most fundamental issue of the research – how effective was the alcohol education package? It will be remembered that the principal objectives of the alcohol education had been formulated in terms of alcohol-related knowledge, attitudes and behaviour. These were measured before and after the educational intervention by means of a questionnaire survey. It was hypothesised that if the alcohol education was effective, there would be significant differences in the post-intervention survey between the young people who had been exposed to the alcohol education and those who had not. Chapter 6 discusses these findings in detail. In general they indicate that the alcohol education package had a small but beneficial impact on the target group. This was particularly evident for knowledge about alcohol, and for consumption behaviour. The impact on attitudes towards alcohol was less clear.

The results of this evaluation study are encouraging especially when placed in the somewhat pessimistic context of evaluating health education in a general sense. In addition, although the impact was limited, the effectiveness was evident in spite of the severe constraints imposed by the research design. Furthermore, effectiveness may be improved when the alcohol education can be implemented with greater flexibility, and integrated into an existing school health education programme and adapted by individual teachers in accordance with their own requirements.

It is unrealistic to expect four hours of alcohol education in the early years of secondary (high) school education to solve all the problems associated with alcohol misuse. Within the context of school, the kind of teaching pack resulting from this study should be seen merely as a 'starter'. The concept of responsible use of alcohol should be developed and reinforced throughout the remainder of compulsory education, and ideally carried on into higher or further education and in the workplace. It is unfair to expect the educational system, be it at the level of primary, secondary or tertiary sectors, to take on, single-handed, the burden of combating the misuse of alcohol amongst young people. Action needs to be co-ordinated at all levels in society, ranging from education within the family to government policy on issues such as price, availability and legal controls.

Examining the role of alcohol education in a wider context, it has been argued that:

> Alcohol education should be an integral part of the work of all health and welfare professionals and should range from prevention in its purest sense – stopping people from ever experiencing problems with alcohol – through to education, which enables the

individual to understand the risks involved and, if required, to modify his behaviour and adopt alternative ways of coping with problems.

(Howe 1989: 47)

However, the current state of affairs in the United Kingdom leaves ample room for improvement. As also noted in the Foreword to the above book:

alcohol education – both about prevention and help – is in a poor state. It is underfunded and professionally has been unrecognised. Training organisations for professional workers are slow to accord alcohol education the prominent place it merits on training schedules. Medical education almost ignores alcohol use and abuse. Elsewhere, attention to this major area is scanty.

(Howe 1989: xi–xii)

Can this situation be improved, and if so, how? Are there lessons to be learned from the experience of others, including countries outside the United Kingdom? In order to examine this possibility, it is necessary to have a general picture of how the problem of educating young people about alcohol, especially in a school setting, is tackled in other countries. In the brief review which follows, the intention is not to provide a representative or even comprehensive selection of alcohol education programmes from around the world. The main purpose is to provide some comparative information which can act as a stimulus to recommendations for improvements and/or alternative strategies within the existing situation in the United Kingdom. While focusing on school-based alcohol education, some attention will be given whenever possible to the links between school and community which facilitate reinforcement of the message about alcohol.

The situation in North America has been commented on by Goodstadt:

Education about drug use has occupied a prominent position in North American school curricula for more than a century. At first, instruction emphasized the risks of alcohol abuse but as the century progressed, began to focus on dangers of illicit drugs. In recent decades there has been a substantial increase in attention given to all forms of drug use, including alcohol and tobacco, as well as use of drugs for medical and non-medical purposes.

(Goodstadt 1986: 278)

Information from Canada suggests that most Boards of Education throughout the nation appreciate the importance of committing curriculum time to education about alcohol and other drugs. In the province of Ontario, for example, the Ministry of Education sets out curriculum guidelines that require health and physical education programmes to include a concentration on alcohol, tobacco and other drugs, beginning at 9 years of age. Various attractively produced resources are available to assist teachers in implementing these guidelines. Examples of these include *Your Health and Alcohol*, produced by Ontario Ministry of Health (1980) for intermediate pupils in Grades 7–10 (aged approximately 13 to 17), and *Positive Life Using Skills* (PLUS) produced by Alcohol and Drug Concerns Inc. targeted at an age range of 9 years (PLUS I) to 17 years (PLUS II) (Burden 1987). Both these programmes emphasise life skills and decision-making, and include explicit information about alcohol. The PLUS II programme covers all psychoactive substances, including prescription drugs. In both packages pupil participation is encouraged, and the materials comprise explanatory notes for teachers and activity/discussion worksheets for pupils. The PLUS programme has as one of its aims the promotion of non-use as a viable alternative. This is reinforced by the provision of weekend 'retreats' for young people where the principal aim is to reinforce the belief that a good time can be had without the aid of alcohol or other drugs.

Also in Canada, in the province of Alberta, the Alberta Alcohol and Drug Abuse Commission (AADAC) launched in 1981 a programme for adolescents which was evaluated in a quasi-experimental setting. This programme is described as a

> long-term, large scale multi-faceted primary prevention program . . . [which] affirms positive adolescent aspirations and subtly illustrates that drinking and drug use could compromise their ability to make the most of their lives. The program focuses on teenage development and adult support rather than on alcohol or drinking *per se*.
>
> (Thompson, J., *et al.* 1987: 10)

Aimed at 12- to 17-year-olds, the programme integrated school, family and mass media approaches to prevention, and included a bi-monthly magazine for adolescents, mailed to their home address. The principal objectives of the campaign were:

Delaying onset of alcohol use
Decreasing frequency and quantity of use

Decreasing use of tobacco and other drugs
Reducing risk associated with alcohol use
Developing health enhancing alternatives to alcohol and drugs.

Survey data collected after the campaign indicates that:

> the percentage of teenage drinkers in Alberta has declined significantly since the introduction of the campaign compared to a control province, Manitoba. Both the frequency of drinking occasions and total quantity consumed by Alberta teenagers has declined.
> (Thomson, J., *et al.* 1987: 10)

Moving to Europe, a wide diversity of approaches is apparent in education for young people about alcohol and other drugs.

In Italy, for example, it has been noted (Monarca 1988) that very few efforts are geared to preventive measures, despite the fact that World Health Organization statistics place Italy among the countries of higher alcohol consumption. In Italy alcohol is inexpensive, readily available and heavily promoted. In 1987, the national mass media were actively involved in a campaign to *promote* wine consumption, using the motto 'Wine is drinking with the heart'. There are no information and/or education campaigns at national level. A small number of school-based and community-based programmes exist at local level, but these are not in any way co-ordinated. One school-based programme for 10- to 12-year-olds was developed at the University of Perugia in the Umbria region of northern Italy. A book of information about alcohol with appropriate references was produced for teachers. This focused on factual information about alcohol and its effects, particularly on the physiological consequences of chronic and heavy drinking. The main emphasis is on the dangers of drinking alcohol and on responses to alcohol-related problems. Teachers are expected to produce their own resource materials based on suggestions in the book.

This example of an alcohol education programme for schools in northern Italy contrasts sharply with the examples from Canada described above. The latter emphasised personal and social development, while the Italian example adopts largely a factual/biological model of alcohol use and misuse and the long-term problems associated with this.

Still in southern Europe, Spain, unlike Italy, does operate restrictive measures to regulate and control mass media advertising of alcohol. In 1988, new legislation in some regions banned the advertising of alcohol and tobacco in public places, including sports stadia, railway stations and airports. At a national level, collaboration between the Ministries of Health and Education resulted in a range of resources for health educators. These include books, leaflets and slides intended for use by family doctors, schoolteachers and social organisations. Although there is no nationally implemented alcohol education programme for schools, some of the autonomous communities in Spain do have their own alcohol and drug prevention programmes for young people. None of these, however, has been subjected to systematic evaluation.

In the Irish Republic, the Health Education Bureau (now the Health Promotion Unit) in Dublin has developed a post-primary school programme which aims 'to provide teachers with specially designed materials to assist them in implementing an alcohol education programme in their schools' (Health Education Bureau 1982). These resource materials, *Living and Choosing – An Approach to Alcohol Education*, comprise factsheets and appropriate visual aids for teachers and activity sheets for pupils. The emphasis is on the development of responsible decision-making skills accompanied by the provision of accurate information about alcohol. Although this resource is intended for use in schools, the overall goal of substance abuse prevention is considered in the context of family and community agencies as well as schools.

In Scandinavia, national concern about alcohol misuse in general is reflected by the existence of state alcohol monopolies which operate strict controls on the availability of alcohol. These differ in the individual Scandinavian countries, and the example discussed here will be restricted to the alcohol retailing monopoly in Sweden – Systembolaget. This company describes itself as a 'state-owned retailing company with no private profit-making interest and special regulations governing operation' (The Swedish Alcohol Retailing Monopoly 1989). The state monopoly restricts availability of alcohol and at the same time provides alcohol information/education. Advertising of alcoholic beverages is permitted only at points of sale, and is thus restricted to restaurants and to the monopoly beverage stores. The monopoly also operates a carefully monitored consumer information programme which has the following aims:

To present the product range impartially
To inform customers about the negative consequences of alcohol consumption and to stimulate moderation through increased knowledge

To encourage people to refrain from alcohol entirely when driving, boating, during pregnancy, when young and in connection with sports and similar situations

To provide information on the current sales rules, particularly the age limit

To popularise non-alcoholic alternatives and to promote a more natural freedom of choice

(Swedish Alcohol Retailing Monopoly 1989: 12)

In Sweden the age limit for the purchase of alcohol in monopoly stores is 20 years, and alcohol consumption by young people is a major concern of the state monopoly. In addition to its internal activities, Systembolaget collaborates with the Swedish mass media to provide information targeted at specific groups. For instance, special campaigns such as 'DON'T BUY ALCOHOL FOR YOUNG PEOPLE' have been run to coincide with annual youth celebrations such as graduation at the end of the school year. Such broad-based campaigns are difficult to evaluate, but information from public opinion polls suggests that they generally achieve high levels of awareness amongst the target population. Of course, as argued throughout this book, increased awareness of risk does not necessarily result in changes in risk-taking behaviours. It is thus interesting to note that, in Sweden, a campaign discouraging alcohol consumption in combination with boating was followed by a decrease in the number of alcohol-related accidents at sea (Hibbel 1988). Caution, however, must be exercised in interpreting an association such as this. As argued throughout this book, failure to employ rigorous evaluation methods means that it is not possible to attribute the reduction in the incidence of alcohol-related accidents at sea solely to the relevant educational intervention. Despite the intuitive appeal of such a conclusion, the issue generally serves to reinforce the need for greater investment of resources in evaluating the impact of preventive measures.

In addition to the countrywide activities of Systembolaget, alcohol education for young people is an integral part of the compulsory health education curriculum in Swedish schools. The Swedish National Board of Education aims to give all teachers access to standard 'service materials' which can be fitted into the centrally-defined syllabus across a variety of subjects in response to local needs. Education about alcohol and/or other drugs is seen to be needed at three levels:

Improving knowledge about drugs
Conditioning pupils' attitudes to drugs
Transforming pupils' behaviour concerning drugs.

These examples of alcohol education from some countries outside the United Kingdom serve to illustrate that there is a wide diversity of approaches and commitment to alcohol education for young people. Some of the more extreme differences are doubtless rooted in the historical and cultural traditions unique to a particular nation. For instance, in the Scandinavian countries, the temperance movement has a long tradition of playing a significant role in national policy and public attitudes to alcohol consumption. In this context severe restrictions on availability and campaigns to moderate consumption are more acceptable to society as a whole. In contrast, in Italy the grape harvest and wine industry play a significant role in the national economy. For this reason, campaigns to reduce problems associated with alcohol misuse, either by restricting availability or by encouraging a reduction in demand, are less likely to be widely acceptable. Social differences of this nature must ultimately have some influence on the commitment to, and provision of, alcohol education in these nations, particularly at a centralised or national level. When considering alcohol education for young people, this is particularly evident in schools.

More specific differences which emerged from the examples above relate to the underlying assumptions and overall objectives of the respective education programmes. In the examples quoted from Canada it was clear that, even within the same province, two of the packages widely available to teachers differed in their ultimate goal. The PLUS programme promotes non-use, and with this overall objective is in a position to include all psychoactive substances in its education materials. The Ministry of Ontario programme, *Your Health and Alcohol*, emphasises individual decision-making skills in order to achieve its goal of advising responsible use of alcohol by young people.

In Italy the school-based education package discussed is largely medical/biological in its approach, and focuses on the physiological harm associated with long-term drug use. Given this factual/informational approach the materials covered a range of psychoactive substances, legal and illegal.

In Sweden, although school-based education about alcohol and other drugs is an essential part of the general health education curriculum, the onus appears to lie ultimately with individual schools to devise their own alcohol education programme. On the other hand, all school-based initiatives about alcohol with a message of responsible use are readily reinforced by the activities of national organisations, often in conjunction with the mass media.

In summary, it is clear that both inside and outside the United Kingdom a wide range of approaches to, and objectives for, alcohol education is to be found. Some educational interventions promote responsible use of alcohol, others have an ultimate goal of non-use. Some cover only alcohol, others refer to alcohol, tobacco and other drugs.

It has already been argued that there is a need in Britain for some kind of standardisation and/or centralisation to encourage the inclusion of alcohol education in the school curriculum, at least in principal. However, any form of centralised supportive structure would have to be established at country level, in order to take account of the very different education systems in Scotland and in England and Wales, with corresponding differences in the organisation of health education. In addition, it was argued that any school-based education about alcohol needs to be reinforced outside the school setting. The overview of some alcohol educational activities outside the United Kingdom in this chapter suggests that this need for co-ordination may be almost universal. In several of the examples discussed above, the aim of the organisation producing the materials for alcohol education has been to provide teachers with a resource which they can adapt for their own purposes. This is excellent, but must be seen as the first rung on the ladder of providing effective alcohol education for young people. Until schools introduce some kind of compulsory health education programme with alcohol education as an integral part of that programme, substance misuse will continue to be the 'poor relation' of the curriculum, its low priority being reflected in little investment in terms of cost or time.

In conclusion, what does the future hold for school-based alcohol education in Britain? As noted in Chapter 1, government concern about alcohol misuse, especially among young people, has been positively expressed in several recent Home Office reports. The recommendations in these reports unanimously identify a need for alcohol education. The important action now is to ensure that these recommendations are followed up, ideally by incorporating, in a nationally-defined curriculum, alcohol education which is based on an approach shown to be effective. Such education modules must at the outset have realistic aims, and must take account of educational philosophy prevalent at the time of implementation. Perhaps the climate in the world of education is ideal for such a change. The 1980s, especially the closing years of the decade, have been a time of substantial change in many aspects of compulsory education. Amongst these, the most relevant to the present discussion is probably the introduction in England and Wales of a core curriculum, the content of which is defined at national level. Sadly, this has not as yet made adequate provision for health education as a subject in its own right. Until this is improved there is a serious danger that alcohol education in English schools, as part of the already low priority health education, will continue to remain absent from many school curricula.

In Scotland, which has an independent education structure, two current activities indicate some optimism for the future. A series of short courses under the heading of Health Studies is available for all 14- to 16-year-olds from 1990. Pupils successfully completing one or more of these forty-hour courses will receive recognition in the Scottish Examination Board's certificate of education. Alcohol education will feature in several of these courses including one which addresses the issue of 'Healthy Risks'. In addition the Scottish Consultative Council on the curriculum, the Secretary of State's advisory body on education, and the Scottish Health Education Group, the national body for health education within the health service, have worked together to produce a joint report *Promoting Good Health – Proposals for Action*. This report considers the management and delivery of health education for 10- to 14-year-olds, an age range which includes the transition from primary to secondary education. The publication will include a report for policy-makers in the teaching profession, covering a range of issues including programme planning, curriculum development, home/school relations and staff training implications. It is also proposed to produce a popular-style publication for parents of those 10- to 14-year-olds, which aims to help them understand the ways in which schools are trying to promote good health.

Activities such as that just described are making admirable attempts to broaden school-based health education outside the classroom, and to engender the support and understanding of parents.

An expansion of this kind of activity would appear to bode well in principle for the future of health education and alcohol education for young people. This is particularly so if such expansion is accompanied by the major recommendations in this book concerning the content, method and proven effectiveness of alcohol education. We may be on the road to success, but at the same time we are becoming more aware of the complexity of the task. There are no easy answers, and there is little doubt that much hard work awaits researchers, teachers and all who work with young people.

Appendix 1a

Alcohol education follow-up questionnaire

Alcohol Research Group
University of Edinburgh

For Office Use Only

Card 1

Respondent Code 1 – 2 – 3 – 4
[ ] [ ] [ ] [ ]

School Code 5 – 6
[ ] [ ]

Stream Code 7
[ ]

Card 1 8
[1]

Educating young drinkers

This questionnaire is the same as the one you completed for us when you were in second year. Do you remember – it is part of a study of what young people like yourselves know and think about alcohol? As last time once you have filled in your answers, we will take the questionnaires away with us, so none of your class-mates or your teachers will see what you have written.

Now we would like you to try and work through the questions on your own. This is not a test or an examination – we just want to know what you really think. Very few of the questions have a right or wrong answer, so please just try to be as honest as you can.

Please PRINT your *full* name clearly below:

_____   _____
        Family Name   First Names

Please PRINT your *full* home address:

_____

_____

_____

What is your date of birth?
   (Write in)
For example:

7	Aug	1973
Date	Month	Year

		19
Date	Month	Year

What is the name of your school?   _____
(Write in)
                    Class: _____

Col. 9

Q.1. Please indicate whether you are male or female: (tick one)

Male		1
Female		2

Col. 10

Q.2. In which country were you born? (tick one)

Scotland		1
England		2
Wales		3
Northern Ireland		4
Irish Republic		5
Elsewhere		6

Col. 11

Q.3. With whom do you live? (tick one)

Mother and father		1
Mother and step-father		2
Father and step-mother		3
Mother only		4
Father only		5
Grandparents		6
Other (specify)		7

Q.4.   Col. 12

(a) What sort of work does your father/step-father usually   1
    do? Write in a few words below to describe this
    work clearly.   2

_____

_____

                                                               Col. 13

(b) Is your father/step-father working | Working | 1
    or unemployed at present? |------------|
    (tick one) | Unemployed | 2

Q.5.   Col. 14

(a) Does your mother/step-mother have a | Yes | 1
    job outside the home? |-----|
    (tick one) | No | 2

(b) *Answer only if she has a job*   Col. 15
    What sort of work does she usually do?
    Write in a few words below to describe this work
    clearly.
                                                                1

_____

                                                                2
_____

                                                               Col. 16

Q.6. Does your father/step-father ever drink | Yes | 1
     alcohol, even just occasionally? |-----|
     (tick one) | No | 2

Follow-up questionnaire

Col. 17

Q.7. Does your mother/step-mother ever drink alcohol, even just occasionally?
(tick one)

| Yes | | 1 |
| No | | 2 |

Col. 18

Q.8. Would your father/step-father mind if you drank alcohol?
(tick one)

Yes		1
No		2
Don't know		3

Col. 19

Q.9. Would your mother/step-mother mind if you drank alcohol?
(tick one)

Yes		1
No		2
Don't know		3

Col. 20

Q.10. Has your father/step-father ever offered you a drink?
(tick one)

| Yes | | 1 |
| No | | 2 |

Col. 21

Q.11. Has your mother/step-mother ever offered you a drink?
(tick one)

| Yes | | 1 |
| No | | 2 |

Col. 22

Q.12. Have you ever fallen out with your parents/step-parents because you have been drinking alcohol?
(tick one)

| Yes | | 1 |
| No | | 2 |

Q.13. Here is a list of different ways which are used to tell people about alcohol. Tick *any* that you have ever had IN YOUR SCHOOL, telling you about alcohol.

	Yes	No	Col.
Film or video			23: 1 2
Leaflet			24: 1 2
Guest speaker			25: 1 2
Slide			26: 1 2
Lesson			27: 1 2
Book			28: 1 2
Other (specify)			29: 1

Q.14. Have you ever been given any information about alcohol or drinking from any of the following people OUTSIDE SCHOOL?

		Yes	No	Col.
(a)	A doctor or a nurse			30: 1 2
(b)	A person from the church			31: 1 2
(c)	A special health visitor			32: 1 2
(d)	Your parents			33: 1 2
(e)	A friend			34: 1 2
(f)	Someone on T.V. or radio			35: 1 2
(g)	Someone in a newspaper or magazine			36: 1 2
(h)	A grandparent			37: 1 2
(i)	Anybody else (write in)			38: 1

Now here is a short quiz about alcohol.

Q.15. Read the following statements. If you think the statement is true, put a tick in the True column. If you think it is false, put a tick in the False column. If you are not very sure, put a tick in the Don't Know column.

	True	False	Don't Know	Col.
(a) Alcohol makes you more alert.				39: 1 2 3
(b) A single whisky (as measured in a pub) is stronger than a pint of beer.				40: 1 2 3
(c) Alcohol is a drug.				41: 1 2 3
(d) The same amount of alcohol affects males and females in the same way.				42: 1 2 3
(e) Eating along with drinking will slow down the effects of alcohol.				43: 1 2 3
(f) Adding soft drinks such as lemonade or fruit juice to alcoholic drinks helps the alcohol to leave the body more quickly.				44: 1 2 3
(g) It is possible to drink small amounts of alcohol without harming health.				45: 1 2 3
(h) Giving alcohol to accident victims can be dangerous.				46: 1 2 3
(i) All lagers and ciders contain roughly the same amount of alcohol.				47: 1 2 3
(j) Drinking only one pint of beer can affect driving skills and the chance of having an accident.				48: 1 2 3
(k) It can be dangerous to drink alcohol if you have taken tablets or medicines.				49: 1 2 3

Question 15 – *continued*

	True	False	Don't Know	Col.
(l) The human body gets rid of two pints of beer in one hour.				50: 1 2 3
(m) Alcohol harms less people in Britain than illegal drugs such as heroin and cocaine.				51: 1 2 3
(n) A glass of table wine contains much more alcohol than half a pint of cider.				52: 1 2 3
(o) Drinking spirits is more likely to lead to problems with alcohol than drinking cider.				53: 1 2 3

For Office Use Only   54   55   56   57
Total A [ ] [ ] Total B [ ] [ ]

Q.16. Have you ever tasted an alcoholic drink; even just a sip?   Col. 58

(for example, cider, shandy, beer, lager, whisky, port, sherry, Guinness, Martini, Babycham, champagne, wine, rum, gin, vodka)
(tick 'Yes' or 'No')

Yes		1
No		2

NOW READ THESE INSTRUCTIONS CAREFULLY

If you have ticked 'Yes', you have tasted even one alcoholic drink, continue with Q.17.

If you have ticked 'no', you have *never* tasted even one alcoholic drink, go to Q.29 on page 15. Do NOT answer questions 17–28.

For People Who Have Ever Tasted An Alcoholic Drink

Q.17. How old were you when you had your first taste of alcohol?   Col. 59

(tick one)

(a) 6 years or younger		1
(b) 7–8 years old		2
(c) 9–10 years old		3
(d) 11–12 years old		4
(e) 13–14 years old		5

Q.18. Who gave you your first taste of alcohol? (tick one)   Col. 60

(a) Parent/step-parent/guardian		1
(b) An *older* brother		2
(c) An *older* sister		3
(d) A brother or sister *not* older than yourself		4
(e) An adult other than parents		5
(f) A boy or girl of your own age (apart from brothers or sisters)		6
(g) Other people – write in		7

Q.19. Below is a list of places where people sometimes have a drink. Tick any of these where you have ever had some alcohol to drink (tick 'Yes' or 'No' for each).

	Yes	No	Col.
(a) In your own home when parents in			61: 1 2
(b) In your own home when parents out			62: 1 2
(c) In the home of adult relatives or friends of your parents			63: 1 2
(d) In a public house or hotel			64: 1 2
(e) In a friend's house when his/her parents in			65: 1 2
(f) In a friend's house when his/her parents out			66: 1 2
(g) At a disco			67: 1 2
(h) In the open air somewhere, such as a street or park			68: 1 2
(i) At a special occasion e.g. a wedding			69: 1 2
(j) Elsewhere – write in			70: 1 2

Q.20. When did you last have any alcohol to drink? (tick one)   Col. 71

Within last week		1
1–2 weeks ago		2
3–4 weeks ago		3
Over 4 weeks – 3 months ago		4
Over 3 months ago		5

Q.21. Whom were you with when you last had some alcohol to drink?
(tick 'yes' or 'no' to each)

	Yes	No	Col.
(a) Parents/step-parents/guardians			72: 1 2
(b) An older brother			73: 1 2
(c) An older sister			74: 1 2
(d) A brother or sister *not* older than yourself			75: 1 2
(e) An adult other than parents			76: 1 2
(f) A boy or girl of your own age apart from brothers or sisters			77: 1 2

For Office Use Only   Card 2

                                  1 – 2 – 3 – 4
              Respondent Code [ ] [ ] [ ] [ ]

                                  5 – 6
              School Code   [ ] [ ]

                                  7
              Stream Code   [ ]

                                  8
              Card 2   [2]

Q.22. Where were you when you last had some alcohol? (tick one)

	Yes	Col. 9
(a) In your own home, with parents		1
(b) In your own home when parents out		2
(c) In the home of *adult* relatives or friends of your parents		3
(d) In a public house or hotel		4
(e) In a friend's house when his/her parents in		5
(f) In a friend's house when his/her parents out		6
(g) At a disco		7
(h) In the open air somewhere, such as a street or park		8
(i) At a special occasion e.g. a wedding		9
(j) Elsewhere – write in where _____		0

Q.23. *Think about the last time you had some alcohol*

Exactly how much did you drink on that occasion?

(a) How much cider, shandy, lager, beer, stout, etc. did you drink? (tick one)   Col. 10

None		1
1 or 2 sips		2
½ – 1 pint		3
1 – 2 pints		4
3 – 4 pints		5
More than 4 pints		6

(b) How many single glasses of Babycham, champagne, wine, Martini, sherry or port did you drink? (tick one)   Col. 11

None		1
1 or 2 sips		2
½ – 1 glass		3
1 – 2 glasses		4
3 – 4 glasses		5
More than 4 glasses		6

(c) How many *single glasses* of whisky, vodka, gin, rum, or other spirits did you drink? (tick one)   Col. 12

None		1
1 or 2 sips		2
½ – 1 glass		3
1 – 2 glasses		4
3 – 4 glasses		5
More than 4 glasses		6

Q.24.

(a) What is the most alcohol you have ever drunk on *one single occasion*? Col. 13

(Write in) _____ 1 2 3

(b) Where did you have this alcohol?
(tick one) Col. 14

At home with parents		1
At home when parents out		2
At a friend's house with parents		3
At a friend's house when parents out		4
At a disco		5
In the open air e.g. street or park		6
Somewhere else – write in		7

(c) How often have you drunk this amount of alcohol?
(tick one) Col. 15

Once only		1
Occasionally		2
Often		3

Q.25. Below is given a list of ways people sometimes feel after they have been drinking. Read through the list, and put a tick to show *if you have ever felt like that* anytime you have been drinking alcohol.

	More than twice	Once or twice	Never	Col.
(a) Happy				16: 1 2 3
(b) Sad				17: 1 2 3
(c) Relaxed				18: 1 2 3
(d) Sick				19: 1 2 3
(e) Feel like smashing things				20: 1 2 3
(f) Feel warm				21: 1 2 3
(g) Feel like a fight or an argument				22: 1 2 3

Q.26. Below is a list of some reasons *why people drink alcohol*. Put a tick by each item to show whether that reason is TRUE or FALSE *for you*.

	True	False	Don't know	Col.
(a) I like the taste				23: 1 2 3
(b) So as not to be the 'odd one out' in a group				24: 1 2 3
(c) To calm my nerves and help me relax				25: 1 2 3
(d) To give myself courage and confidence				26: 1 2 3
(e) It helps me to talk to members of the opposite sex more easily				27: 1 2 3
(f) So that my friends won't think I'm scared or 'yellow'				28: 1 2 3
(g) To help me mix more easily with other people				29: 1 2 3
(h) To help me stop worrying about something				30: 1 2 3
(i) Because my friends all drink				31: 1 2 3
(j) Because it's an adult thing to do				32: 1 2 3
(k) To look good in front of other people				33: 1 2 3
(l) To find out what it's like				34: 1 2 3

Q.27.   Col. 35

(a) Do you think you have ever had a hangover? | Yes | | 1
    (tick one) | No | | 2

(b) How many times have you had a hangover *in the last six months*?

Col. 36

Never		1
Once only		2
2 – 3 times		3
4 – 5 times		4
Over 5 times		5

Q.28. Please tick 'yes' or 'no' to *each* of the following questions:

		Yes	No	Col.
(a)	Have you ever been told off by adults for drinking alcohol?			37: 1 2
(b)	Have you ever had problems at school because you have been drinking alcohol?			38: 1 2
(c)	Have you ever spent more money than you should on drink?			39: 1 2
(d)	Have you ever had trouble or quarrels with family or friends because you have been drinking alcohol?			40: 1 2
(e)	Have you ever had money problems because of your drinking?			41: 1 2
(f)	Have you ever had an accident or hurt yourself after drinking alcohol?			42: 1 2
(g)	Have you ever arrived late for school due to a hangover?			43: 1 2
(h)	Have you ever missed a day's school due to a hangover?			44: 1 2
(i)	Have you ever had an upset stomach because of drinking?			45: 1 2
(j)	Has your drinking ever worried you?			46: 1 2
(k)	Has your drinking ever caused you problems?			47: 1 2
(l)	Have you ever felt guilty or ashamed about your drinking?			48: 1 2

NOW GO TO QUESTION 32.
MISS OUT QUESTIONS 29 TO 31.

ONLY ANSWER QUESTIONS 29–31 IF YOU HAVE NEVER TASTED AN ALCOHOLIC DRINK.

Q.29. Read through the questions below and then put a tick by each one to show *how often* these have happened to you.

	Often	Sometimes	Never	Col.
(a) If someone offers you some alcohol have you ever been tempted to try it?				49: 1 2 3
(b) When you are at a party or disco where some people are drinking alcohol do you ever feel 'left out' of things?				50: 1 2 3
(c) Do your friends ever urge you to try 'just a little one', or try to persuade you to have a drink?				51: 1 2 3

128   Educating young drinkers

Q.30. Below is a list of some reasons why people do *NOT* drink. Read through the list and tick each item to show whether that reason is TRUE or FALSE *for you*.

	True	False	Col.
(a) I dislike the taste.			52: 1 2
(b) Drinking is bad for you.			53: 1 2
(c) Drinking costs too much.			54: 1 2
(d) People who drink are unpleasant.			55: 1 2
(e) Drinking is against my religion.			56: 1 2
(f) Drinking makes people lose control of themselves.			57: 1 2
(g) Once you start drinking you can't stop the habit.			58: 1 2
(h) My parents disapprove strongly of anyone who drinks.			59: 1 2
(i) I want to be fit.			60: 1 2
(j) Drinking makes you put on weight.			61: 1 2
(k) Some other reason (write what). _____ _____			62: 1 2

Col. 63

Q.31. Do you think you may sometimes drink alcohol when you get older? (tick one)	Yes		1
	No		2
	Don't know		3

ALL THE REMAINING QUESTIONS SHOULD BE ANSWERED BY EVERYONE.

Q.32. Have you ever tried any of the following either from curiosity or for 'kicks'?
(tick 'yes' or 'no' for each).

	Yes	No	Col.
(a) Cannabis ('pot', marijuana, 'dope', 'grass', 'hash', 'ganja')			64: 1 2
(b) LSD ('acid')			65: 1 2
(c) Barbiturates			66: 1 2
(d) Glues, solvents (by sniffing)			67: 1 2
(e) Amphetamines (pep pills, 'speed')			68: 1 2
(f) Opium			69: 1 2
(g) Morphine			70: 1 2
(h) Heroin			71: 1 2
(i) Cocaine or Crack			72: 1 2
(j) Sleeping tablets/tranquillizers (e.g. Ativan, Mogadon, Librium, Valium)			73: 1 2
(k) Other drugs (write what) _____ _____			74: 1 2

130 Educating young drinkers

Col. 75

Q.33. Have you ever tried smoking tobacco?
(a) (either in cigarettes, cigars or a pipe)
(tick one)

Yes		1
No		2

(b) About how many cigarettes do you smoke now? Col. 76
(tick one)

None		1
One a week or fewer		2
2–4 per week		3
5–10 per week		4
11–20 per week		5

(c) If a friend offered you a cigarette would you smoke it? Col. 77
(tick one)

Yes		1
No		2
Don't know		3

For Office Use Only　　　　　　　　　Card 3

　　　　　　　　　　　　　　　1 – 2 – 3 – 4
　　　　　　Respondent Code　[ ] [ ] [ ] [ ]

　　　　　　　　　　　　　　　5 – 6
　　　　　　School Code　　　[ ] [ ]

　　　　　　　　　　　　　　　7
　　　　　　Stream Code　　　[ ]

　　　　　　　　　　　　　　　8
　　　　　　Card 3　　　　　　[3]

Q.34. Finally, here is a list of statements about alcohol. Put a tick for each statement to show whether *you* agree or disagree with it. Only use the 'Not Sure' box if you are completely stuck. Please try to be as honest as you can.

	Agree	Disagree	Not Sure	Col.
(a) People who drink alcohol are never lonely.				9: 1 2 3
(b) Buying alcohol is a waste of money.				10: 1 2 3
(c) Even one drink can lead to trouble.				11: 1 2 3
(d) Teenagers who drink alcohol are more adult than those who don't.				12: 1 2 3
(e) A little alcohol makes a party go better.				13: 1 2 3
(f) Young people who drink alcohol are more likely to get into trouble at school.				14: 1 2 3
(g) Alcohol makes people bad-tempered.				15: 1 2 3
(h) Young men are silly to think it's 'tough' to drink alcohol.				16: 1 2 3
(i) People who never drink alcohol are a bit odd.				17: 1 2 3
(j) Teenagers who drink alcohol are more attractive.				18: 1 2 3
(k) Alcohol causes football hooliganism.				19: 1 2 3
(l) People who drink alcohol are usually scruffy and untidy.				20: 1 2 3
(m) Teenagers who drink alcohol have lots of friends of the opposite sex.				21: 1 2 3

132 Educating youg drinkers

Question 34 – *continued*

	Agree	Dis-agree	Not Sure	Col.
(n) Teenagers who never drink are more popular with adults.				22: 1 2 3
(o) Alcohol makes people more fun to be with.				23: 1 2 3
(p) When teenagers drink alcohol they usually end up fighting.				24: 1 2 3
(q) Teenagers who drink alcohol have a more exciting social life than teenagers who don't drink.				25: 1 2 3
(r) People who don't drink are nicer people than drinkers.				26: 1 2 3
(s) Alcohol makes people more friendly.				27: 1 2 3
(t) The law should be changed to allow younger people to buy alcohol.				28: 1 2 3

Total P
29 30
[ ] [ ]

Total N
31 32
[ ] [ ]

THANK YOU VERY MUCH FOR YOUR HELP IN COMPLETING THIS QUESTIONNAIRE.

Now that you have answered all the questions in this questionnaire, try not to disturb the others who have not yet finished.

Just for fun, have a go at the word game on the next page.

WORD GAME

Here is a list of words. Draw a line through all the ones you can find in the squares below. Each word may occur in any direction.

- Pineapple
- Orange juice
- Ice
- Spirits
- Tumblers
- Alcohol
- Lemon
- Lime
- Soft drinks
- Water
- Cocktail
- Glasses
- Jug
- Grapefruit
- Cherry
- Olives

A	L	E	C	I	U	J	E	G	N	A	R	O
L	I	C	B	C	R	E	L	I	M	E	R	R
C	N	I	N	X	P	A	N	C	Y	A	N	A
O	A	R	O	F	S	P	I	R	P	L	T	N
S	L	I	M	S	P	I	R	P	I	J	U	G
K	E	P	E	C	H	E	B	I	N	A	M	R
N	L	S	L	L	H	E	R	N	W	O	B	A
I	P	C	O	C	O	C	K	T	A	I	L	P
R	P	H	W	A	T	H	G	A	T	C	E	E
D	A	S	E	V	I	L	O	I	E	E	R	F
T	E	P	A	P	P	E	L	C	R	U	S	R
F	N	I	L	R	O	M	E	E	L	P	A	U
O	I	R	G	L	A	O	V	U	I	A	O	I
S	P	I	R	I	T	S	E	R	B	M	U	T

If you like, you may tear this page off before handing in your questionnaire.

Appendix 1b
Addsyg ar alcohol ail holiadur

Grŵp Ymchwil ar Alcohol
Prifysgol Caeredin

At ddefnydd y swyddfa'n unig Cerdyn 1

                            1 – 2 – 3 – 4
              Côd yr atebwr [ ] [ ] [ ] [ ]

                            5 – 6
              Côd yr ysgol [ ] [ ]

                            7
              Côd y ffrwd   [ ]

                            8
              Cerdyn 1   [1]

Mae'r holiadur hwn yr un fâth a hwnnw a gwblhawyd gennych yn yr ail flwyddyn. A ydych yn ei gofio – mae yn rhan o astudiaeth sy'n ymchwilio i'r hyn y mae pobl ifainc fel chi yn ei wybod a'i feddwl am alcohol. Wedi ichi ateb y cwestiynau, byddwn yn mynd â'r holiaduron gyda ni rhag i'ch cyd-ddisgyblion weld eich atebion.

Nawr, hoffwn ichi roi cynnig ar ateb y cwestiynau ar eich pen eich hun. Nid prawf nag arholiad yw hwn – yr hyn rydym eisiau ei wybod yw beth yn gwmws yr ydych yn ei feddwl am alcohol. Ychydig iawn o'r cwestiynau sydd ag atebion cywir neu anghywir iddyn nhw, felly triwch fod mor onest a diffuant â phosibl.

Ysgrifennwch eich enw'n llawn mewn LLYTHRENNAU BREISION isod:

Enw Teulu   Enwau Cyntaf

Ysgrifennwch eich cyfeiriad cartref yn llawn mewn LLYTHRENNAU BREISION:

Beth yw'ch dyddiad geni?
(Llenwch y blychau)
Er enghraifft:

7	Awst	1973

Dydd Mis Blwyddyn

		19
Dydd	Mis	Blwyddyn

Beth yw enw'ch ysgol?
(Ysgrifennwch)
           Dosbarth:

Addsyg ar alcohol ail holiadur 137

Col. 9

C.1. Nodwch os ydych

Bachgen		1
Merch		2

Col. 10

C.2. Ym mha wlad y'ch ganed chi?
(ticiwch un blwch)

Yr Alban		1
Lloegr		2
Cymru		3
Gogledd Iwerddon		4
Gweriniaeth Iwerddon		5
Rhywle arall		6

Col. 11

C.3. Gyda phwy ydych chi'n byw?

Tad a mam		1
Mam a llystad		2
Tad a llysfam		3
Mam yn unig		4
Tad yn unig		5
Tadcu a/neu famgu		6
Eraill (manylwch)		7

138   Educating young drinkers

C.4. Col. 12

(a) Pa fath o waith y mae'ch tad/llystad yn ei wneud fel 1
arfer? Disgrifiwch yn glir mewn ychydig eiriau isod y
gwaith hwn. 2

_____

_____

_____

Col. 13

(b) A yw'ch tad/llystad yn gweithio

| Yn gweithio | | 1 |
| Yn ddiwaith | | 2 |

neu a yw'n ddiwaith ar hyn o
bryd? (ticiwch un blwch)

C.5. Col. 14

(a) A oes swydd gyda'ch mam/llysfam
y tu allan i'r cartref?
(ticiwch un blwch)

| Oes | | 1 |
| Nac oes | | 2 |

(b) *Atebwch dim ond os oes swydd gyda hi.* Col. 15
Pa fath o waith y mae'n ei wneud fel arfer?
Disgrifiwch yn glir mewn ychydig eiriau isod y gwaith
yma.

  1

_____

  2

_____

_____

Col. 16

C.6. Ydy'ch tad/llystad yn yfed alcohol o
gwbl hyd yn oed os mai dim ond yn
achlysurol?

| Ydy | | 1 |
| Nac ydy | | 2 |

Col. 17

C.7. Ydy'ch mam/llysfam yn yfed alcohol o gwbl, hyd yn oed os mai dim ond yn achlysurol?

Ydy		1
Nac ydy		2

Col. 18

C.8. A fyddai ots gyda'ch tad/llystad pe baech yn yfed alcohol? (ticiwch un blwch)

Byddai		1
Na fyddai		2
Ddim yn gwybod		3

Col. 19

C.9. A fyddai ots gyda'ch mam/llysfam pe baech yn yfed alcohol? (ticiwch un bwlch)

Byddai		1
Na fyddai		2
Ddim yn gwybod		3

Col. 20

C.10. A ydy'ch tad/llystad wedi cynnig diod ichi erioed?

Ydy		1
Nac ydy		2

Col. 21

C.11. A ydy'ch mam/llysfam wedi cynnig diod ichi erioed? (ticiwch un blwch)

Ydy		1
Nac ydy		2

Col. 22

C.12. A ydych wedi cwympo mas â'ch rhieni/llysrieni am ichi yfed alcohol? (ticiwch un blwch)

Ydw		1
Nac ydw		2

C.13. Dyma restr o'r gwahanol ffyrdd a ddefnyddir i ddweud wrth bobl am alcohol. Ticiwch y rheiny 'rydych wedi'u cael YN YR YSGOL, yn sôn am alcohol.

	Ydw	Nac ydw	Col.
Ffilm neu fideo			23: 1 2
Taflen			24: 1 2
Siaradwr gwadd			25: 1 2
Sleidiau			26: 1 2
Gwers			27: 1 2
Llyfr			28: 1 2
Arall (manylwch)			29: 1

C.14. A ydych wedi derbyn gwybodaeth am alcohol neu am yfed gan unrhyw un o'r canlynol y TU ALLAN I'R YSGOL?

		Ydw	Nac ydw	Col.
a.	Doctor neu nyrs			30: 1 2
b.	Person o'r eglwys			31: 1 2
c.	Ymwelydd iechyd arbennig			32: 1 2
ch.	Eich rhieni			33: 1 2
d.	Cyfaill			34: 1 2
dd.	Rhywun ar y teledu neu'r radio			35: 1 2
e.	Rhywun mewn papur neu gylchgrawn			36: 1 2
f.	Tadcu neu Famgu			37: 1 2
ff.	Rhywun arall (manylwch)			38: 1

Nawr, dyma gwis bach am alcohol.
C.15. Darllenwch y sylwadau a ganlyn. Os ydych yn credu'u bod yn wir, rhowch dic yn y golofn 'Gwir'. Os nad ydych yn credu'u bod yn wir, rhowch dic yn y golofn 'Gau'.

	Gwir	Gau	Ddim yn gwybod	Col.
a. Mae alcohol yn eich gwneud yn fwy bywiog.				39: 1 2 3
b. Mae un wisgi (mesur tafarn) yn gryfach na peint o gwrw.				40: 1 2 3
c. Cyffur yw alcohol				41: 1 2 3
ch. Mae'r un faint o alcohol yn cael yr un faint o effaith ar ddynion a menywod.				42: 1 2 3
d. Mae bwyta ac yfed yr un pryd yn lleddfu ar effeithiau'r alcohol.				43: 1 2 3
dd. Mae ychwanegu diodydd meddal fel lemonêd a sudd ffrwythau at ddiodydd alcoholig yn helpu'r alcohol i adael y corff yn gynt.				44: 1 2 3
e. Mae'n bosibl yfed tameidiau bach o alcohol heb niweidio'r iechyd.				45: 1 2 3
f. Mae'n beryglus rhoi alcohol i bobl sydd newydd gael damwain.				46: 1 2 3
ff. Mae tua'r un faint o alcohol ym mhob sidir a lager.				47: 1 2 3
g. Gall yfed ond un peint o gwrw effeithio ar eich gallu i yrru ac i osgoi damweiniau.				48: 1 2 3

Gwestiwn 15 (– *continued*)

	Gwir	Gau	Ddim yn gwybod	Col.
ng. Gall yfed alcohol ar ôl cymryd tabledi neu foddion fod yn beryglus.				49: 1 2 3
h. Mae'r corff dynol yn cael gwared ar ddau beint o gwrw mewn awr.				50: 1 2 3
i. Mae alcohol yn niweidio llai o bobl ym Mhrydain nag yw cyffuriau anghyfreithlon megis heroin, cocain.				51: 1 2 3
l. Ceir llawer mwy o alcohol mewn gwydraid o win bwrdd nag a geir mewn hanner peint o sidir.				52: 1 2 3
ll. Mae'n fwy tebygol y cewch broblemau ag alcohol o yfed gwirodydd nag o yfed sidir.				53: 1 2 3

At ddefnydd y swyddfa'n unig   54   55   56   57
Cyfanswm A [ ] [ ]   Cyfanswm B [ ] [ ]

C.16. A ydych wedi blasu un llwnc hyd yn oed, o ddiod alcoholig erioed? (e.e. sidir, shandy cwrw, lager, wisgi, port, sieri, Guinness, Martini, Babycham, champagne, gwin, rwm, gin, fodca).
(Ticiwch 'Ydw' neu 'Nac ydw')

Col. 58

| Ydw | | 1 |
| Nac ydw | | 2 |

NAWR, DARLLENWCH Y CYFARWYDDIADAU HYN YN OFALUS

Os gwnaethoch dicio 'Ydw', sef eich bod wedi blasu diod alcoholig, ewch ymlaen at C.17.

Os gwnaethoch dicio 'Nac ydw', sef *nad* ydych wedi blasu diod alcoholig erioed yn eich bywyd, ewch at C.29 ar dud. 16. PEIDIWCH ag ateb cwestiynau 17 – 28.

Ar Gyfer Pobl Sydd Wedi Blasu Diod Alcoholig

C.17. Beth oedd eich oedran pan gwnaethoch flasu alcohol gyntaf? (ticiwch un blwch)

Col. 59

a.	6 blwydd neu lai		1
b.	7 – 8 blwydd oed		2
c.	9 – 10 blwydd oed		3
ch.	11 – 12 blwydd oed		4
d.	13 – 14 blwydd oed		5

C.18. Gan bwy y cawsoch eich blas cyntaf o alcohol? (ticiwch un blwch)

Col. 60

a.	Rhiant/llysriant/gwarcheidwad		1
b.	Brawd *hŷn*		2
c.	Chwaer *hŷn*		3
ch.	Brawd neu chwaer nad yw'n hŷn na chi		4
d.	Oedolyn ac eithrio rhiant		5
dd.	Bachgen neu ferch yr un oedran â chi (ar wahân i'ch brodyr neu chwiorydd)		6
e.	Pobl eraill – manylwch		7

C.19. Isod, rhestrir llefydd y mae pobl weithiau'n yfed ynddynt. Ticiwch y rheiny yr ydych wedi yfed alcohol ynddynt. (Ticiwch 'Do' neu; 'Naddo' i bob un)

		Do	Naddo	Col.
a.	Yn eich cartref pan mae'ch rhieni i mewn			61: 1 2
b.	Yn eich cartref pan mae'ch rhieni allan			62: 1 2
c.	Yng nghartref perthnasau mewn oed neu ffrindiau'ch rhieni			63: 1 2
ch.	Mewn tafarn neu westy			64: 1 2
d.	Yng nghartref eich ffrind pan fydd ei rieni/rhieni i mewn			65: 1 2
dd.	Yng nghartref eich ffrind pad fydd ei rieni/rhieni allan			66: 1 2
e.	Mewn disgo			67: 1 2
f.	Yn yr awyr agored yn rhywle, fel stryd neu barc			68: 1 2
ff.	Ar achlysyr arbennig e.e. priodas			69: 1 2
g.	Yn rhywle arall – manylwch			70: 1 2

C.20. Pryd cawsoch unrhyw alcohol i'w yfed ddiwethaf?
(ticiwch un blwch)   Col. 71

O fewn yr wythnos ddiwethaf		1
1–2 wythnos yn ôl		2
3–4 wythnos yn ôl		3
Dros 4 wythnos – 3 mis yn ôl		4
Dros 3 mis yn ôl		5

C.21. Gyda phwy beddech chi pan gawsoch ddiod ddiwethaf?
(ticiwch 'Ie' neu 'Nage' ar gyfer pob blwch)

		Ie	Nage	Col.
a.	Rhieni/llysrieni/gwarcheidwaid			72: 1 2
b.	Brawd hŷn			73: 1 2
c.	Chwaer hŷn			74: 1 2
ch.	Brawd neu chwaer nad yw'n hŷn na chi			75: 1 2
d.	Oedolyn ac eithrio rhieni			76: 1 2
dd.	Bachgen neu ferch yr un oedran â chi (ar wahân i'ch brodyr neu chwiorydd)			77: 1 2

At ddefnydd swyddfa'n unig   Cerdyn 2

                               1 - 2 - 3 - 4
           Côd yr Atebwr   [ ]   [ ]   [ ]   [ ]

                               5 - 6
           Côd yr Ysgol   [ ]   [ ]

                               7
           Côd y Ffrwd   [ ]

                               8
           Cerdyn 2   [2]

C.22. Ble oeddech chi pan gawsoch alcohol ddiwethaf?
(ticiwch un blwch)

		Do	Naddo	Col. 9
a.	Yn eich cartref pan mae'ch rhieni i mewn			1
b.	Yn eich cartref pan mae'ch rhieni allan			2
c.	Yng nghartref perthnasau mewn oed neu ffrindiau'ch rhieni			3
ch.	Mewn tafarn neu westy			4
d.	Yng nghartref eich ffrind pan fydd ei rieni/rhieni i mewn			5
dd.	Yng nghartref eich ffrind pan fydd ei rieni/rhieni allan			6
e.	Mewn disgo			7
f.	Yn yr awyr agored yn rhywle, fel stryd neu barc			8
ff.	Ar achlysyr arbennig e.e. priodas			9
g.	Yn rhywle arall – manylwch			0

C.23. *Meddyliwch am y tro diwethaf ichi gael alcohol*

Faint yn gwmws a wnaethoch ei yfed ar yr achlysur hwnnw?

a. Faint o sidir, shandy, lager, cwrw, stowt, ac ati a wnaethoch ei yfed? (ticiwch un blwch) Col. 10

Dim	1
1 neu 2 lwnc	2
$\frac{1}{2}$ - 1 peint	3
1 - 2 beint	4
3 - 4 peint	5
Mwy na 4 pheint	6

b. Sawl *gwydraid sengl* o Babycham, champagne, gwin, Martini, sieri neu port a wnaethoch ei yfed (ticiwch un blwch) Col. 11

Dim	1
1 - 2 lwnc	2
$\frac{1}{2}$ - 1 gwydraid	3
1 - 2 wydraid	4
3 - 4 gwydraid	5
Mwy a 4 gwydraid	6

c. Sawl gwydraid sengl o wisgi, fodca, gin, rwm neu wirodydd eraill wnaethoch ei yfed? (ticiwch un blwch) Col. 12

Dim	1
1 - 2 lwnc	2
$\frac{1}{2}$ - 1 gwydraid	3
1 - 2 wydraid	4
3 - 4 gwydraid	5
Mwy na 4 gwydraid	6

C.24.

a. Beth yw'r swm mwyaf o alcohol ichi ei yfed erioed *ar un achlysur*?   Col. 13

   (Manylwch) _____   1 2 3

b. Ble cawsoch chi'r alcohol yma?
   (ticiwch un blwch)   Col. 14

Adref gyda'ch rhieni		1
Adref â'ch rhieni allan		2
Yng nghartref ffrindiau gyda'u rhieni		3
Yng nghartref ffrindiau â'u rhieni allan		4
Mewn disgo		5
Yn yr awyr agored e.e. stryd, parc		6
Yn rhywle arall – manylwch		7

c. Sawl gwaith ydych wedi yfed cymaint â hyn o alcohol?
   (ticiwch un blwch)   Col. 15

Unwaith yn unig		1
Yn achlysurol		2
Yn aml		3

C.25. Rhestrir isod sut mae pobl weithiau'n teimlo wedi iddyn nhw fod yn yfed. Darllenwch y rhestr a rhowch dic i ddweud *os yr ydych wedi teimlo fel yna erioed* unrhyw bryd wedi ichi fod yn yfed alcohol.

		Yn aml	O dro i dro	Byth	Col.
a.	Yn hapus				16: 1 2 3
b.	Yn drist				17: 1 2 3
c.	Wedi ymlacio				18: 1 2 3
ch.	Yn dost				19: 1 2 3
d.	Yn teimlo awydd i chwalu pethau				20: 1 2 3
dd.	Yn teimlo'n gynnes				21: 1 2 3
e.	Yn teimlo awydd i ymladd neu ddadlau				22: 1 2 3

C.26. Isod, rhestrir rhai o'r rhesymau *pam mae pobl yn yfed* alcohol. Ticiwch bob eitem i ddangos pas reswm sy'n WIR neu'n GAU *yn eich achos chi*.

		Gwir	Gau	Ddim yn Gwybod	Col.
a.	Rwy'n hoffi'r blas				23: 1 2 3
b.	Er mwyn cael gwneud yr un peth â phawb arall mewn grŵp				24: 1 2 3
c.	I dawelu fy nerfau a'm helpu i ymlacio				25: 1 2 3
ch.	I roi hyder a dewrder imi				26: 1 2 3
d.	Mae'n fy helpu i siarad ag aelodau'r rhyw arall				27: 1 2 3
dd.	Rhag i'm ffrindiau feddwl fod ofn arnaf neu fy mod yn 'gachgi'				28: 1 2 3
e.	I'm helpu i ddod ymlaen yn well â phobl eraill				29: 1 2 3
f.	Rhag imi boeni am rywbeth				30: 1 2 3
ff.	Gan fod fy ffrindiau i gyd yn yfed				31: 1 2 3
g.	Am ei fod yn rhywbeth y mae oedolion yn ei wneud				32: 1 2 3
ng.	Er mwyn edrych yn dda o flaen eraill				33: 1 2 3
h.	Er mwyn cael gwybod sut fath o beth ydyw				34: 1 2 3

C.27. Col. 35

a. A ydych wedi cael pen tost ar ôl meddwi erioed? (ticiwch un blwch)

Ydw		1
Nac ydw		2

b. Sawl gwaith ydych chi wedi cael pen tost ar ôl meddwi *yn ystod y chwe mis diwethaf?*

Col. 36

Byth		1
Unwaith yn unig		2
2 – 3 gwaith		3
4 – 5 gwaith		4
Mwy na 5 gwaith		5

C.28. Ticiwch 'Do' neu 'Naddo' ar gyfer pob cwestiwn:

		Do	Naddo	Col.
a.	A ydych wedi cael pryd o dafod gan oedolion am ichi yfed alcohol erioed?			37: 1 2
b.	A greuwyd problemau ichi yn yr ysgol am ichi yfed alcohol?			38: 1 2
c.	A wnaethoch wario mwy nag y dylech ar yfed erioed?			39: 1 2
ch.	A gawsoch helbul neu gweryl erioed gyda'ch teulu neu'ch ffrindiau am ichi fod yn yfed alcohol?			40: 1 2
d.	A greuwyd problemau ariannol gan eich yfed?			41: 1 2
dd.	A gawsoch ddamwain neu ddolur erioed ar ôl yfed alcohol?			42: 1 2
e.	A wnaethoch gyrraedd yr ysgol yn hwyr erioed am fod pen tost ar ôl meddwi arnoch?			43: 1 2
f.	A wnaethoch golli diwrnod o ysgol am fod pen tost ar ôl meddwi arnoch?			44: 1 2
ff.	A gawsoch fola tost erioed am ichi fod yn yfed?			45: 1 2
g.	A fu'ch yfed yn destun pryder ichi erioed?			46: 1 2
ng.	A greuir problemau ichi gan eich yfed?			47: 1 2
h.	A wnaethoch deimlo'n euog neu a fuodd cywilydd arnoch oherwydd eich yfed?			48: 1 2

NAWR, EWCH YMLAEN AT GWESTIWN 32.
PEIDIWCH AG ATEB CWESTIYNAU 29-31.

ATEBWCH GWESTIYNAU 29-31 OS NAD YDYCH WEDI BLASU DIOD ALCOHOLIG ERIOED.

C.29. Darllenwch y cwestiynau isod a rhowch dic wrth bob un i ddangos *pa mor aml* y maent wedi digwydd ichi.

	Yn aml	O dro i dro	Byth	Col.
a. Os oes rhywun wedi cynnig alcohol ichi, ac a ydych wedi cael eich temtio i dderbyn?				49: 1 2 3
b. Os ydych mewn parti neu ddisgo lle mae rhai pobl wrthi'n yfed alcohol, ydych chi'n teimlo eich bod 'allan' ohoni?				50: 1 2 3
c. A ydy'ch ffrindiau yn eich cymell i drio 'un bach', neu'n trio eich perswadio i gael diod?				51: 1 2 3

C.30. Isod, rhestrir rhai o'r rhesymau pam NAD yw pobl yn yfed. Darllenwch y rhestr a ticiwch bob eitem i ddangos a yw'r rheswm hwnnw'n WIR neu'n GAU *yn eich achos chi.*

		Gwir	Gau	Col.
a.	Dwi ddim yn hoffi'r blas			52: 1 2
b.	Mae yfed yn ddrwg ichi			53: 1 2
c.	Mae yfed yn rhy ddrud			54: 1 2
ch.	Mae pobl sy'n yfed yn annymunol			55: 1 2
d.	Mae yfed yn erbyn fy naliadau crefyddol			56: 1 2
dd.	Mae yfed yn gwneud i bobl golli gafael arnynt eu hunain			57: 1 2
e.	Unwaith ichi ddechrau yfed, mae'n anodd rhoi'r gorau iddi			58: 1 2
f.	Mae fy rhieni yn gwrthwynebu yfed			59: 1 2
ff.	Rwy am fod yn heini			60: 1 2
g.	Mae yfed yn gwneud ichi roi pwysau ymlaen			61: 1 2
ng.	Rhyw reswm arall (manylwch)			62: 1 2

C.31. Ydych chi'n credu y gwnewch chi yfed alcohol weithiau pan fyddwch yn hŷn (ticiwch un bwlch)   Col. 63

Ydw		1
Nac ydw		2
Ddim yn gwybod		3

DYLAI PAWB ATEB Y CWESTIYNAU SY'N WEDDILL

C.32. A ydych wedi rhoi cynnig ar y canlynol, naill ai oherwydd chwilfrydedd neu am 'sbort'? (ticiwch 'ydw' neu 'nac ydw' am bob un)

		Ydw	Nac ydw	Col.
a.	Cannabis ('pot', marihuana, 'dôp', 'gwair', 'grass', 'hash', 'ganja')			64: 1 2
b.	LSD ('asid', diethylamid asid lysergaidd/25)			65: 1 2
c.	Barbituradau			66: 1 2
ch.	Gludion, toddyddion (trwy ffroeni)			67: 1 2
d.	Amphetaminau (pep pills, spīd)			68: 1 2
dd.	Opiwm			69: 1 2
e.	Morffin			70: 1 2
f.	Heroin			71: 1 2
ff.	Cocain neu Crac			72: 1 2
g.	Tabledi Cysgu/Tawelyddion (e.e. Ativan, Mogadon, Librium, Valium)			73: 1 2
ng.	Cyffuriau eraill (manylwch)			74: 1 2

C.33. A ydych wedi trio smygu baco erioed? Col. 75
(a) (naill ai mewn sigaret, sigâr neu bîb)
(ticiwch un bwlch)

| Ydw | | 1 |
| Nac ydw | | 2 |

(b) Sawl sigaret ydych chi'n smygu nawr? Col. 76
(ticiwch un blwch)

Dim		1
Un yr wythnos neu lai		2
2–3 yr wythnos		3
5–10 yr wythnos		4
11–20 yr wythnos		5

(c) Pe bai cyfaill yn cynnig sigaret ichi, a fyddech yn ei smygu? (ticiwch un blwch) Col. 77

Buaswn		1
Na fuaswn		2
Ddim yn gwybod		3

At ddefnydd y swyddfa'n unig   Cerdyn 3

                                   1 – 2 – 3 – 4
                    Côd yr Atebwr [ ] [ ] [ ] [ ]

                                   5 – 6
                    Côd yr Ysgol   [ ] [ ]

                                   7
                    Côd y Ffrwd   [ ]

                                   8
                    Cerdyn 3   [3]

C.34. I gloi, dyma restr o sylwadau am alcohol. Rhowch dic wrth y sylwadau i ddangos a ydych *chi* yn cytuno â hwy ai peidio. Ticiwch y blwch 'Ddim yn Siŵr' os na fedrwch benderfynu un ffordd neu'r llall. Ceisiwch fod mor onest â phosibl.

		Cytuno	Anghytuno	Ddim yn Siŵr	Col.
a.	Nid yw pobl sy'n yfed alcohol fyth yn unig.				9: 1 2 3
b.	Mae prynu alcohol yn wastraff ar arian.				10: 1 2 3
c.	Gall un diod hyd yn oed arwain at helynt.				11: 1 2 3
ch.	Mae pobl ifainc sy'n yfed alcohol yn fwy aeddfed na'r rheiny nad ydynt yn gwneud.				12: 1 2 3
d.	Mae ychydig o alcohol yn rhoi hwb i barti.				13: 1 2 3
dd.	Mae pobl ifainc sy'n yfed alcohol yn fwy tebygol o fynd i helynt yn yr ysgol.				14: 1 2 3
e.	Mae alcohol yn gwneud pobl yn ddrwg eu hwyl.				15: 1 2 3
f.	Mae dynion ifainc yn dwp i feddwl bod yfed alcohol yn beth 'caled'.				16: 1 2 3
ff.	Mae pobl nad ydynt fyth yn cyffwrdd ag alcohol braidd yn rhyfedd.				17: 1 2 3
g.	Mae pobl ifainc sy'n yfed alcohol yn fwy deniadol.				18: 1 2 3
ng.	Mae alcohol yn achosi hwliganiaeth ymysg cefnogwyr peldroed.				19: 1 2 3

C.34. – *continued*

		Cytuno	Anghy-tuno	Ddim yn Siwr	Col.
h.	Mae pobl sy'n yfed alcohol fel arfer yn anniben a diraen.				20: 1 2 3
i.	Mae gan bobl ifainc sy'n yfed alcohol lawer o ffrindiau o'r rhyw arall.				21: 1 2 3
l.	Mae oedolion yn meddwl yn fwy o bobl ifainc nad ydynt yn yfed alcohol.				22: 1 2 3
ll.	Mae alcohol yn gwneud pobl yn fwy o sbort.				23: 1 2 3
m.	Mae pobl ifainc sy'n yfed alcohol, fel arfer yn mynd i ymladd.				24: 1 2 3
n.	Mae gan bobl ifainc sy'n yfed alcohol fywydau cymdeithasol mwy bywiog na'r rheiny nad ydynt yn gwneud.				25: 1 2 3
o.	Mae pobl nad ydynt yn yfed alcohol yn bobl fwy dymunol na'r rheiny sydd yn gwneud.				26: 1 2 3
p.	Mae alcohol yn gwneud pobl yn fwy serchus.				27: 1 2 3
ph.	Dylid newid y gyfraith er mwyn i bobl ifainc allu prynu alcohol.				28: 1 2 3

DIOLCH O GALON AM GWBLHAU'R HOLIADUR.

```
                                29   30
                    Cyfanswm P [  ] [  ]
                                31   32
                    Cyfanswm N [  ] [  ]
```

Addsyg ar alcohol ail holiadur 159

Gan eich bod nawr wedi ateb holl gwestiynau'r holiadur, peidiwch â tharfu ar y rheiny nad ydynt eto wedi dibenu.

Am hwyl, rhowch gynnig ar y gêm geiriau ar y dudalen nesaf.

GEM GEIRIAU

Dyma restry o eiriau. Tynnwch linell drwy bob un gallwch ddod o hyd iddo yn y sgwar isod. Gall y geiriau fod mewn unrhyw gyfeiriad.

gwîn
oren
gwydr
alcohol
ceirios
grawnwin
cnau
dŵr

tafarn
lemon
cwrw
meddw
jwg
diodydd
cyren duon
gwesty

dd	l	t	o	n	y	w	g	w	y	d	r	b
s	c	a	ff	a	o	î	n	î	n	a	d	î
î	i	f	o	u	r	a	n	s	c	m	ch	o
d	n	a	g	w	e	s	t	y	dd	e	t	f
d	ŵ	r	o	a	n	dd	r	c	a	dd	a	ff
ŵ	o	n	l	d	o	e	a	e	g	w	î	n
t	l	e	m	o	n	l	t	i	a	r	c	i
w	e	g	w	d	i	o	dd	r	e	n	y	w
c	n	a	u	ŵ	t	y	d	i	g	w	j	n
c	n	o	i	n	d	i	o	o	r	n	o	w
w	n	t	r	o	i	ŵ	i	s	a	w	e	a
r	w	l	i	n	a	l	c	o	h	o	l	r
w	j	d	dd	y	d	e	i	o	s	i	w	g

Os y mynnwch, gallwch dynnuir dudalen hon allan cyn choi'ch holiadur i mewn.

Appendix 2
Statistical analyses used in evaluation study

This appendix provides some details of the statistical analyses used in the evaluation study described in this book.

The principal hypothesis of this evaluation study was that exposure to the alcohol education package would lead to changes in the alcohol-related knowledge, attitudes and behaviour of the 12- to 13-year-olds in the target group. The hypothesis was tested by using a controlled study design with pre- and post-intervention measures as described in Chapter 2. The principal statistical analysis involved comparing the young people in the two intervention groups (t_1 and t_2 in Figure 2.2) with those in the control group (C in Figure 2.2). In order to establish that any differences arising between these groups were not merely due to chance, but could be attributed to the educational intervention, analysis of variance was carried out using a three-by-three factorial model. This is illustrated in Figure A.1 following.

Figure A.1 Three-by-three factorial model

Experimental group		Region*		
	r_1	r_2	r_3	
C	cell 1			C
t_1				T_1
t_2				T_2
	R_1	R_2	R_3	Total

Note: * Region: r_1 = Highland; r_2 = Berkshire; r_3 = Dyfed
Experimental group: t_1 = 'non-specialist' intervention
t_2 = 'specialist' intervention
C = control

Each cell in the grid of Figure A.1 represents individual schools in the study so that, for example, cell 1 will always contain the data for the control group school in region 1. This model enables the main effects of region and experimental group to be tested against the interaction effect. In addition, orthogonal comparison was used (see Guilford and Fruchter 1978) to split the group effect and so enable statistical testing of the difference between C (control group) and T_1 plus T_2 (combined intervention groups). Similarly it was possible to compare T_2 (the 'specialist' intervention groups) with T_1 (the 'non-specialist' intervention groups).

In the main text it was noted that significance levels were set at $p<0.01$, unless otherwise stated. The statistically alert reader may have noticed that in Chapter 6 some of the results of the evaluation study were quoted at a less significant level. This was done because the overall research design of the study resulted in a small number of degrees of freedom in the subsequent analyses. This in turn restricted the sensitivity of the F-tests using the above factorial model. For evaluation of the educational intervention, the unit of analysis is the individual school. The degrees of freedom, and therefore the sensitivity of the F-tests could have been increased by using more schools in the study (possibly with fewer pupils in each school). However, such statistical considerations have to be offset against the practical constraints of fieldwork and data collection in studies of this kind.

Bibliography

Aaro, L.E., Bruland, E., Hauknes, A. and Lochsen, P.M. (1983) 'Smoking among Norwegian schoolchildren 1975–1980. III. The effect of anti-smoking campaigns', *Scandinavian Journal of Psychology* 24: 277–83.

Ahlström, S. (1987) 'Young people's drinking habits' in J. Simpura (ed.) *Finnish Drinking Habits*, Finnish Foundation for Alcohol Studies, 35: 135–49.

Ahlström, S. (1988) 'A comparative study of adolescent drinking habits', Paper given at 1st Annual Meeting of Kettil Bruun Society for Social and Epidemiological Research on Alcohol, Berkeley, California.

Aitken, P.P., Leathar, D.S. and Scott, A.C. (1988) '10–16 year olds' perceptions of advertisements for alcoholic drinks', *Alcohol and Alcoholism* 23(6): 491–500.

Ajzen, I. and Fishbein, M. (1980) *Understanding Attitudes and Predicting Social Behavior*, Englewood Cliffs, New Jersey: Prentice-Hall.

Akers, R. (1968) 'Teenage drinking – a survey of action programs', paper at University of Washington, Institute for Sociological Research.

Anderson, D. (ed.) (1989) 'The current debate about alcohol: extreme allegations and sobering evidence', in *Drinking to Your Health – The Allegations and the Evidence*, London: Social Affairs Unit.

Bacon, M. and Jones, M. (1968) *Teenage Drinking*, New York: Crowell.

Bagnall, G.M. (1988) 'Use of alcohol, tobacco and illicit drugs amongst 13-year-olds in three areas of Britain', *Drug and Alcohol Dependence* 22: 241–51.

Bagnall, G.M. (1990) *Alcohol Education – A Teaching Pack*, London: Hodder & Stoughton.

Bagnall, G.M. and Plant, M.A. (1987) 'Education on drugs and alcohol: past disappointments and future challenges', *Health Education Research* 2(4): 417–422.

Bannister, D. and Salmon, P. (1975) 'A personal construct view of education', *New York University Education Quarterly* 6(4): 28–31.

Botvin, G. (1982) 'Broadening the focus of smoking prevention strategies', in T. Coates, A. Peterson and C. Perry (eds) *Promoting Adolescent Health*, New York: Academic Press.

Burden, K. (1987) *PLUS II: An Alcohol/Drug Prevention Program*, Ontario: Alcohol and Drug Concerns, Inc.

Cohen, S. (1972) *Folk Devils and Moral Panics*, London: Granada.
Crawford, A. (1987) 'Bias in a survey of drinking habits', *Alcohol and Alcoholism* 22(2): 167-79.
Crawford, A., Plant, M., Kreitman, N. and Latcham, R. (1987) 'Unemployment and drinking behaviour: some data from a general population survey of alcohol use', *British Journal of Addiction* 82: 1007-16.
Davies, J.B. and Stacey, B. (1972) *Teenagers and Alcohol: A Developmental Study in Glasgow*, vol. 2, London: HMSO.
De Haes, W.F.M. (1987) 'Looking for effective drug education programmes: 15 years explanation of the effects of different drug education programmes', *Health Education Research – Theory and Practice* 2(4): 433-8.
De Haes, W.F.M. and Schuurman, J.H. (1975) 'Results of an evaluation study of three drug education methods', *International Journal of Health Education* 18: 1-16.
Department of Health and Social Security (1982) *Treatment and Rehabilitation: Report of the Advisory Council on the Misuse of Drugs*, London: HMSO.
Dobbs, J. and Marsh, A. (1984) *Smoking Among Secondary School Children in 1984*, London: HMSO.
Duffy, J. (1989) 'Total alcohol consumption in a population and alcohol-related problems', in D. Anderson (ed.) *Drinking to Your Health – The Allegations and the Evidence*, London: The Social Affairs Unit.
Dunbar, J. (1985) *The Quiet Massacre*, Occasional Paper no. 7, London: Institute of Alcohol Studies.
Evans, R.I., Rozelle, R.M., Mittelmark, M.B., Hansen, W.B., Bane, A.L. and Havis, J. (1978) 'Deterring the onset of smoking in children: knowledge of immediate physiological effects and coping with peer pressures, media pressure and parent modelling', *Journal of Applied Social Psychology* 8: 126-36.
Farrant, W. and Russell, J. (1986) *The Politics of Health Information*, Bedford Way Paper no. 28, London: Institute of Education, University of London.
Fazey, C. (1977) *The Aetiology of Psychoactive Substance Use*, Paris: UNESCO.
Finn, P. (1977) 'Alcohol education and the pleasures of drinking', *Health Education* 8(1): 17-19.
Fishbein, M. (1980) 'A theory of reasoned action: some applications and implications', in H. Howe and M. Page (eds) *Nebraska Symposium on Motivation 1979*, Lincoln, Nebraska: University of Nebraska Press.
Fontane, P. and Layne, N. (1979) 'The family as a context for developing youthful drinking patterns', *Journal of Alcohol and Drug Education* 24: 19-29.
Ghodsian, M. and Power, C. (1987) 'Alcohol consumption between the ages of 16 and 23 in Britain: a longitudinal study', *British Journal of Addiction* 82(2): 175-80.
Gillies, P. (1986) 'Preventing smoking in schoolchildren', unpublished PhD thesis, University of Nottingham.
Gillies, P. and Wilcox, B. (1984) 'Reducing the risk of smoking amongst the young', *Public Health* 98: 49-54.
Goddard, E. and Ikin, C. (1987) *Smoking Among Secondary School Children*, London: HMSO.
Goodstadt, M. (1986) 'School-based drug education in North America: what is wrong? What can be done?' *Journal of School Health* 56(7): 278-81.

Gordon, N. and McAlister, A. (1982) 'Adolescent drinking: issues and research', in T. Coates, A. Petersen and C. Perry (eds) *Promoting Adolescent Health*, New York: Academic Press.

Grant, M. (1982) 'Young people and alcohol problems: educating for individual and social change', Paper given at 10th International Congress of the International Association for Child and Adolescent Psychiatry and Allied Professions, July.

Grant, M. (1986) 'Comparative analysis of the impact of alcohol education in North America and western Europe', in T. Babor (ed.) *Alcohol and Culture – Comparative Perspectives from Europe and North America* 472: 198–210, New York Academy of Sciences.

Grant, M. and Ritson, B. (1983) *Alcohol: The Prevention Debate*, London: Croom Helm.

Green, L. (1979) 'National policy in the promotion of health', *International Journal of Health Education* 22(3): 161–8.

Grube, J. and Morgan, M. (1986) 'Smoking, drinking and other drug use among Dublin post-primary school children', Report for The Economic and Social Research Institute, Dublin.

Guilford, J.P. and Fruchter, B. (1978) *Fundamental Statistics in Psychology and Education*, Tokyo: McGraw-Hill Kogakuska.

Hamburg, B. (1989) 'Adolescent health care and disease prevention in the Americas', in D. Hamburg and N. Sartorius (eds) *Health and Behaviour*, Cambridge University Press.

Hansen, A. (1986) 'T.V. and public images of alcohol', Paper presented at Research Symposium on Addictive Behaviours, University of Dundee, March.

Hansen, W.B., Johnson, C.A., Flay, B.R., Graham, J.W. and Sobel, J. (1988) 'Affective and social influences approaches to the prevention of multiple substance abuse among 7th grade students: Results from Project SMART', *Preventive Medicine* 17: 135–54.

Health Education Bureau (now Health Promotion Unit) (1982) *Living and Choosing – An Approach to Alcohol Education*, Dublin: Ministry of Health.

Health Education Studies Unit (1982) *Final Report on the Patient Project (September 1977 to November 1982)*, London: Health Education Council (now Health Education Authority).

Heien, D. and Pittman, D. (1989) 'The economic costs of alcohol abuse: an assessment of current methods and estimates', *Journal of Studies on Alcohol* 50(6): 567–76.

Hibbel, B. (1985) 'Adolescent drinking and drinking problems in Sweden', Paper given at International Symposium on Extent and Nature of Adolescent Alcohol Use, Washington, July.

Hibbel, B. (1988) 'Alcohol education in Sweden – a country report', Paper given at annual meeting of the Alcohol Education Section Core Group, International Council on Alcohol and the Addictions, Italy, October.

Home Office (1984) *Prevention: Report of the Advisory Council on the Misuse of Drugs*, London: HMSO.

Home Office (1985) *Tackling Drug Misuse: A Summary of the Government's Strategy*, London: HMSO.

Home Office Standing Conference on Crime Prevention (1987) *Report*

of the Working Group on Young People and Alcohol, London: Crown Office.
Howe, B. (1989) *Alcohol Education: A Handbook for Health and Welfare Professionals*, London: Tavistock/Routledge.
Jackson, P.M. (1989) 'Estimating the social costs of alcohol abuse', in D. Anderson (ed.) *Drinking to Your Health – The Allegations and the Evidence*, London: The Social Affairs Unit.
Jahoda, G. and Cramond, J. (1972) *Children and Alcohol: A Developmental Study in Glasgow*, vol. 1, London: HMSO.
Jessor, R. (1982) 'Critical issues in research on adolescent health promotion', in T. Coates, A. Petersen and C. Perry (eds) *Promoting Adolescent Health*, New York: Academic Press.
Jessor, R. and Jessor, S. (1977) *Problem Behaviour and Psychosocial Development: A Longitudinal Study of Youth*, New York: Academic Press.
Johnston, L., Bachman, J. and O'Malley, P. (1977) *Drug Use Among American High School Students, 1975–1977*, Report prepared by Institute for Social Research for National Institute on Drug Abuse.
Kelly, G.A. (1970) 'Behaviour as an experiment', in D. Bannister (ed.) *Perspectives in Personal Construct Theory*, London: Academic Press.
Kinder, B.N., Pape, N.E. and Walfish, S. (1980) 'Drug and alcohol education programmes: a review of outcome studies', *International Journal of the Addictions* 15: 1035–54.
Kreitman, N. (1986) 'Alcohol consumption and the preventive paradox', *British Journal of Addiction* 81: 353–63.
Ledwith, F. and Osman, L. (1985) 'The evaluation of a secondary school smoking education intervention', *Health Education Journal* 44: 131–3.
McAlister, A.L. (1982) 'Drugs and Alcohol – Introduction and Overview', in T. Coates, A. Petersen and C. Perry (eds) *Promoting Adolescent Health – A Dialog on Research and Practice*, London: Academic Press.
McAlister, A.L., Perry, C., Killen, J., Slinkard, L.A. and Maccoby, N. (1980) 'Pilot study of smoking, alcohol and drug abuse prevention', *American Journal of Public Health* 70: 719–25.
McAlister, A.L., Perry, C. and Maccoby, N. (1979) 'Adolescent smoking: onset and prevention', *Pediatrics* 63: 650–58.
McDonnell, R. and Maynard, A. (1985) 'The costs of alcohol misuse', *British Journal of Addiction* 80(1): 27–36.
McKennel, A.C. (1980) 'Bias in the reported incidence of smoking by children', *International Journal of Epidemiology* 9(2): 167–77.
Marsh, A. (1984) *Smoking: Habit or Choice? Population Trends 14–20*, London: HMSO.
Marsh, A., Dobbs, J. and White, A. (1986) *Adolescent Drinking*, London: HMSO.
Milgram, G. (1987) 'Alcohol and drug education programs', *Journal of Drug Education* 17(1): 43–57.
Ministry of Health (1980) *Your Health and Alcohol*, Ontario.
Monarca, S. (1988) 'Alcohol education in Italy – a country report', Paper given at annual meeting of the Alcohol Education Section Core Group, International Council on Alcohol and the Addictions, Italy, October.
Naidoo, J. (1986) 'Limits to individualism', in S. Rodmell and A. Watt (eds) *The Politics of Health Education. Raising the Issues*, London: Routledge & Kegan Paul.

O'Connor, J. (1978) *The Young Drinkers*, London: Tavistock.
O'Connor, J. (1985) 'Adolescent drinking and drinking problems in Ireland', Paper given at International Symposium on Extent and Nature of Adolescent Alcohol Use, Washington, July.
Olafsdottir, H. (1985) 'Adolescent drinking in Iceland', Paper given at International Symposium on Extent and Nature of Adolescent Alcohol Use, Washington, July.
Peck, D.F. (1982) 'Some determining factors', in M.A. Plant (ed.) *Drinking and problem drinking*, London: Junction.
Pernanen, K. (1974) 'Validity of survey data on alcohol use', in R.J. Gibbons, Y. Israel, H. Kalant, R.E. Popham, W. Schmidt and R.G. Smart (eds) *Research Advances in Alcohol and Drug Problems*, vol. 1, New York: John Wiley.
Petersen, A. (1982) 'Developmental issues in adolescent health', in T. Coates, A. Petersen and C. Perry (eds) *Promoting Adolescent Health — A Dialog on Research and Practice*, London: Academic Press.
Plant, M.A. (1981) 'What aetiologies?' in G. Edwards and C. Busch (eds) *Drug Problems in Britain*, London: Academic Press.
Plant, M.A. (1987) *Drugs in Perspective*, London: Hodder & Stoughton.
Plant, M.A., Peck, D.F. and Samuel, E. (1985) *Alcohol, Drugs and Schoolleavers*, London: Tavistock.
Pope, M. and Keen, T.R. (1981) *Personal Construct Psychology and Education*, London: Academic Press.
Rachal, J.V., Williams, J.R., Brehm, M.L., Cavanaugh, B., Moore, R.P. and Eckermann, W.C.A. (1975) *A National Study of Adolescent Drinking Behavior, Attitudes and Correlates*, Report prepared for National Institute on Alcohol Abuse and Alcoholism, Springfield, VA.
Royal College of General Practitioners (1986) *Alcohol — A Balanced View*, Report from General Practice 24, London.
Royal College of Physicians (1987) *A Great and Growing Evil: The Medical Consequences of Alcohol Abuse*, London: Tavistock.
Royal College of Psychiatrists (1986) *Alcohol: Our Favourite Drug*, London: Tavistock.
Sales, J., Duffy, J., Plant, M.A. and Peck, D.F. (1989) 'Alcohol consumption, cigarette sales and mortality in the United Kingdom: an analysis of the period 1970–1985', *Drug and Alcohol Dependence* 24: 155–60.
Samuel, E. (1984) 'Alcohol education in schools: assessing the scope for constraints upon new initiatives', Paper given at Alcohol Epidemiology Symposium, International Council on Alcohol and the Addictions, Edinburgh.
Schaps, E., Dibartolo, R., Moskowitz, J., Balley, C.G. and Churgin, G. (1981) 'A review of 127 drug abuse prevention programme evaluations', *Journal of Drug Issues* 11: 17–43.
Schools Council/Health Education Council Project (1984) *Health Education 13–18*, London: Forbes Publications.
Scottish Health Education Group (1985) *So You Want to Cut Down Your Drinking? A Self-help Guide to Sensible Drinking*.
Secondary Science Curriculum Review (1983) *An Outline of the Purpose, Organisation and Operation of the Review*, London: Schools Council Publications.

Smart, R. (1989) 'Increased exposure to alcohol and cannabis education and changes in use patterns', *Journal of Drug Education* 19(2): 183–94.
Spring, J. and Buss, D. (1977), cited in *Alcohol – A Balanced View*, Royal College of General Practitioners, London: 1986: 5.
Stuart, R. (1974) 'Teaching facts about drugs: pushing or preventing?' *Journal of Educational Psychology* 66(2): 189–201.
Swedish Alcohol Retailing Monopoly (1989) *A Presentation of Systembolaget*, Stockholm.
Swisher, J.D., Crawford, J., Goldstein, R. and Yura, M. (1971) 'Drug education: pushing or preventing?' *Peabody Journal of Education* 49: 68–75.
Teachers' Advisory Council on Alcohol and Drug Education/Health Education Council (1984) *Alcohol Education Syllabus 11–16*.
Tether, P. (1989) 'Liquor licensing: theory, practice and potential', in D. Anderson (ed.) *Drinking to Your Health – The Allegations and the Evidence*, London: The Social Affairs Unit.
Thompson, J., Skirrow, J., and Nutter, C. (1987) 'The AADAC prevention program for adolescents: achieving behavior change', Paper given at 33rd International Institute on the Prevention and Treatment of Alcoholism, Lausanne, June.
Tones, K. (1987a) 'Role of the health action model in preventing drug abuse', *Health Education Research – Theory and Practice* 2(4): 305–16.
Tones, K. (1987b) 'Health education, PSE and the question of voluntarism', *Journal of the Institute of Education* 25(2): 41–52.
Triandis, H.C. (1980) 'Values, attitudes and interpersonal behavior', in H. Howe and M. Page (eds) *Nebraska Symposium on Motivation 1979*, Lincoln, Nebraska: University of Nebraska Press.
Vartiainen, E., Pallonen, U., McAlister, A., Koskela, K. and Puska, P. (1986) 'Four-year follow-up results of the smoking prevention program in the North Karelia Youth Project', *Preventive Medicine* 15: 692–8.
Winton, M., Heather, N. and Robertson, I. (1986) 'Effects of unemployment on drinking behaviour: a review of the relevant evidence', *International Journal of the Addictions* 21(12): 1261–83.
World Health Organization (1982) *Alcohol Consumption and Alcohol-Related Problems: Development of National Policies and Programmes*, Report on Technical Discussions of 35th World Health Assembly, Geneva: WHO.

Index

Aaro, L.E. 22
absenteeism, alcohol and 5
abstinence: age and 54–5; stigmatised 24–5; total 66; transition to drinking 54
accidents: domestic 5; road traffic 11
activities in alcohol education package 67–9, 78–9
activity-based learning 63
addiction, stereotypes of 7
adolescence: drinking behaviour, and adult consumption 28, 31; gender and consumption 10; parental influence in 10; perspective of 63; ritual passage to adulthood 15; skills, in drug education 28; *see also* study group; youth
adulthood, symbols of 15
advertisements, alcohol: analysis of 68; control of 102–3; salient features 9; size 76
Advisory Council on the Misuse of Drugs 7–8
affective education, effectiveness 27
age: and abstinence 54–5; and alcohol education 83–4; of initiation 55–6, 57–8; of target group, selection 66
Ahlström, S. 11, 54, 55, 57, 58
Aitken, P.P. 9
Ajzen, I. 13
Akers, R. 10

Alberta Alcohol and Drug Abuse Commission (AADAC) 101–2
alcohol: advertisements 68, 76, 102–3; availability 5; experience of 42–4, 48–52, 83; information about 44–5, 51, 67, 79, 80, 96; licensing regulations 5; price 2, 5, 8; taxation 5; uses of 1, 5
alcohol consumption: and absenteeism 5; and accidents 5, 11; in adolescence 28; alcohol education package and 92; amounts 96; attitudes to 46, 52, 92; control group 90, 91, 92; cultural influences and 11; economic factors and 8; effects of 45, 51, 58, 59, 64, 68, 77, 96; family context 96; frequency of 48, 57–8, 96; gender and 10–11, 58; halving 6; immorality of 24; increased 2, 80, 83, 93–9; initiation 29, 42, 55–8; levels 5, 6; long-term effects 64, 68; maximum 43–4; mind-altering qualities xiv; parental attitudes to 46; patterns of 1, 6, 7–12, 48–54; portrayal 9; positive aspects of 24–5, 67–8; reasons for 7–12; regular 83; responsible, enjoyment of 68; social factors in 8–10; transition from abstinence 54; under-age 11–12; United Kingdom 1–7; *see also* misuse
alcohol education: age and 83–4; aims 28–9; approach to 29;

Index

assessed 23–5; communication modes 25; co-ordination 106; credibility 24; in curriculum 106–7; definition xv; drug education, separate from 74; educational emphasis of 59; effective 19, 23–5; evaluation 15, 94; fear tactics 24; harm minimisation 26; heavy drinkers and 24; important features 32, 61–2; and increased consumption 80, 93–4; low priority 46–7, 93; in national curriculum 106–7; and personal experience 63, 68; as political issue 16; as primary intervention xv, xvi; relevance 24; resource materials xv, xvi, 39; responsibility, developing 59, 66; risk reduction 19, 26; role 99–100; school-based xv–xvi, 17; single-lesson programmes 25; and social change 18; social influences approach 68; specific behaviour approach 29; targeting 83

alcohol education package: activities in 67–9, 78–9; administration 84; aims 66–7, 93; alcohol consumption and 92; assessment 84, 98–9; changes after piloting 69–70; colour reproduction 69, 70, 76; consistency of 62; content 64; context 62; cost 81; description 65–70; development 35, 39–40, 84; developmental stage 64; feedback 71–82, 98; first steps 61–2; follow-up study 35, 85–94, 109–33; health education in 81; individual participation 63; key issues 32, 61–2; length 70, 92, 93; materials 81, 98; methods 63–4; needs of consumers 61; objectives 96; open-ended activities 63; piloting 40, 69–70; positive effect 91–2, 99; relevance 96; research and experimental perspective 97; staffing 65; as 'starter' 99; success 81, 93, 94; target population 64–5; teacher's manual 65–7, 73, 98; topics, possible 74

alcohol education research project 29–30; aims 32, 95; baseline survey 35, 41–59, 83–4, 96; data collection 38; feedback 71–82; follow-up survey 35, 84–94; main study 32–3; method design 33–5; pilot study 32; positive effect 91–2, 99; questionnaire (Appendix 1a) 38, 39, 41; selection of schools 35–8; statistical analysis 160–1; study areas 33, 34; survey instrument 38; Welsh language questionnaire (Appendix 1b) 38, 39, 41

alcohol misuse 59; controls on 5–6; epidemiological triangle 13–14, 23; and other drugs 28; prevalence xiv; prevention xv; and problem behaviour 12–13; reasons for 7–12; social costs of 5; stereotypes of 9

Alcohol Research Group, Edinburgh University xvi, 75, 77, 78; Lothian study 31–2, 37, 38, 54, 69–70, 93

alcoholic drinks: definition 55; relative strengths 67, 98

alcohol-related attitudes: changes in 89–90, 91; and knowledge 90; positive 92; study group 46, 52

alcohol-related behaviour, changes in 27, 90–1, 99

alcohol-related knowledge: changes in 86–9; gender differences 88–9; improved 86, 92, 99

alcohol-related problems 5; policy responses to 5–6

Anderson, D. 5

Argentina, alcohol consumption 4

attitudes, alcohol-related: changes in 89–90, 91; and knowledge about alcohol 90; positive 90; study group 46, 52

Australia, alcohol consumption 4

Austria, alcohol consumption 4

Bacon, M. 10
Bagnall, G.M. 11, 20, 28, 65, 67, 69, 81
Bannister, D. 63
barriers to healthy behaviour 14
baseline survey 35, 41–59, 83–4, 96; compared with other studies 54–9; and follow-up survey 85–94
beer, British consumption of 2, 3
behaviour: changes in 27, 90–1, 99; intentions 13
Belgium, alcohol consumption 4
Berkshire alcohol education research project 33
Bible, alcohol in xiv
Botvin, G. 21
Brazil, alcohol consumption 4
Britain *see* United Kingdom
Bulgaria, alcohol consumption 4
Burden, K. 101
Buss, D. 2

Cameroon, alcohol consumption 4
Canada: alcohol consumption 4; alcohol education 24, 101; cannabis education 22–3
cannabis education 22–3
cartoon-based humour 69
case studies, fictitious 68, 75
Chile, alcohol consumption 4
choices, making 67, 78
cider, British consumption of 2, 3
cigarette smoking 21–2, 47–8; sex differences 58; social acceptability 19, 21; *see also* tobacco education
class teachers, feedback from 75–7
Cohen, S. 7
Columbia, alcohol consumption 4
contaminated data 87
content: of alcohol education package 64; of health education package 61; relevance of 68
context: alcohol education package 62; of health education package 61; of initiation 56
'contracting out' option 37

control group 36; alcohol consumption 90, 91, 92; contamination 87, 88; health education 20
control, locus of 18
coping skills 27
core curriculum: alcohol education in 107; health education in 73
coronary heart disease, prevention 16
Cramond, J. 97
Crawford, A. 8, 38
Cuba, alcohol consumption 4
cultural influences, and consumption 11
curriculum: alcohol education in 62; core 73, 107; national 106–7
Czechoslovakia, alcohol consumption 4

data: collection 38; contaminated 87; self-reported 38
Davies, J.B. 10
De Haes, W.F.M. 13, 20, 23, 25, 26
decision-making 67
Denmark, alcohol consumption 4
developmental stage, target group 62, 64
diary, seven-day 42
Dobbs, J. 22
drinking *see* alcohol consumption
drug education: approaches to 23; effectiveness 22–3, 27; implementation process 27–8; and increased drug use 25, 27; ineffective 21; separate from alcohol education 74; and total prevention 26
drug use, illicit: legal substitutes for 15; and other drugs 48; school's responsibility 66; tobacco and 59
Dublin, alcohol education 103
Duffy, J. 6
Dunbar, J. 11
Dyfed alcohol education research project 33, 38, 39, 41

economic factors and alcohol consumption 8

Edinburgh University Alcohol
  Research Group xvi, 75, 77, 78;
  Lothian study 31–2, 37, 38, 54,
  69–70, 93
Edinburgh workshop 39, 65
education: and alcohol misuse xv;
  see also alcohol education
educational administrators, and
  alcohol education 32
education programmes, effectiveness
  13–14
effects of alcohol consumption 59,
  77, 96; sex differences 58
employment status and alcohol use
  8
England and Wales: age and
  abstinence 54–5; frequency of
  consumption 57; road traffic
  accidents 11; see also United
  Kingdom
epidemiological triangle 13–14, 23
ethnic origin and youthful drinking
  behaviour 10
European Community, alcohol
  consumption 2, 3, 4
evaluation: methodology 96;
  statistical analyses 160–1
Evans, R.I. 21
experience of alcohol 83; increased
  85; sex differences in 48–52;
  study group 42–4, 85–6

family, influence of 10
family context: alcohol consumption
  96; of initiation 56
Farrant, W. 16, 17
father, influence of 10
Fazey, C. 8
fear-arousal approaches 24, 26;
  ineffective 21, 24
Feedback Forms: and questionnaire
  98
feedback: pupils 77–80, 98;
  teachers 72–7, 98
females: adolescent alcohol
  consumption 11, 49, 50, 51; age
  of initiation 57; attitudes about
  alcohol 52; consequences of
  alcohol consumption 51;
frequency of consumption 48, 50,
  51, 57–8; knowledge about
  alcohol 51, 88–9; reasons for
  consumption 51–2; tobacco use
  52–3, 58
fictitious case studies 68, 75
film material, use 72–3, 75, 76
Finland: age of initiation 55;
  alcohol consumption 4; frequency
  of consumption 58; gender and
  alcohol consumption 11, 58;
  skills-based approach 26
Finn, P. 24, 68
first taste see initiation
Fishbein, M. 13
follow-up study 35, 109–33;
  baseline survey and 85–94
Fontane, P. 10
France, alcohol consumption 2, 4
frequency of alcohol consumption
  57, 58, 96; sex differences 48–51,
  58
friends, influence of 10, 11, 68, 97

gender, and alcohol consumption
  10–11, 57–8; and experience of
  alcohol 48–52
German DR, alcohol consumption
  4
German FR, alcohol consumption
  4
Ghodsian, M. 28
Gillies, P. 22, 26, 92
Glasgow, youth and advertisements
  9
Goddard, E. 19, 58
Goodstadt, M. 27–8, 100
Gordon, N. 10, 24, 28, 55, 56
Grant, M. 8–9, 15, 23, 25
Great Britain see United Kingdom
Greece, alcohol consumption 2, 4
Green, L. 17
Grube, J. 13
Guidance curriculum 62

Hamburg, B. 15, 20
Hansen, A. 9
Hansen, W.B. 26, 92
Health Action Model 14

health defined 60
health education: aims 60; alcohol education package in 81; approaches to 23, 26–7; basic prerequisite 16; control group 20; in core curriculum 73; criticism of 16; defined 17; effectiveness 20–8, 95–6; and increased use 23, 25, 27, 80; individualistic 16–17, 60–1; low priority 93, 106; objectives 16; package xiv, 61–2; politics of 16; role of schools 60; for social change 18; social influences approach 26–7; specific behaviour approach 29; studies, evaluation 20
Health Education Bureau 103
Health Education Council (HEC) xv, 60, 61
Health Education Studies Unit 63
health promotion, defined 17
Health and Social Security, Department of 6–7
healthy behaviour, barriers to 14
heavy drinkers and alcohol education 24
Heien, D. 5
heroin education, fear tactics 26
Hibbel, B. 56, 104
high-gloss reproduction 70, 77
Highland alcohol education research project 33
Home Office 7, 8, 11–12
Howe, B. 100
humour, use of 69
Hungary, alcohol consumption 4

Iceland, context of initiation 56
Ikin, C. 19, 58
income and alcohol use 8
individualistic health education 16–17, 60–1
information about alcohol 79, 80, 96
information approach to drug education 23, 25
initiation: age of 55–6, 57–8; context of 56–7; and later development 29; parental 42, 56
intervention group schools 37

intoxication: effects of 58; occasional 83; risks of 59, 64, 67
Irish Republic: alcohol consumption 2, 4; alcohol education 103; context of initiation 56
Italy: alcohol consumption 4, 102; alcohol education 102, 105; preventive measures 102; wine industry, importance 105

Jackson, P.M. 5
Jahoda, G. 97
Japan, alcohol consumption 4
Jessor, R. 12, 29–30, 63
Jessor, S. 12, 63
Johnston, L. 11, 55, 58
Jones, M. 10

Keen, T.R. 63
Kelly, G.A. 63
Kenya, alcohol consumption 4
Kinder, B.N. 20, 25
knowledge, alcohol-related 67; changes in 86–9; improved 86, 92, 99; sex differences 51, 88–9; study group 44–5
Korea, alcohol consumption 4
Kreitman, N. 6

Layne, N. 10
Ledwith, F. 22
life skills 18, 21, 26
Living and Choosing – An Approach to Alcohol Education 103
locus of control 18
Lothian region study 31–2, 37, 38; abstainers 54; and alcohol education 93; contracting-out option 37; schools 69–70

McAlister, A.L. 10, 21, 24, 28, 55, 56
McKennel, A.C. 38
main study 32–3
males: adolescent alcohol consumption 11; age at initiation 51, 57; attitudes about alcohol 52; effects of alcohol consumption 51, 52, 96;

frequency of consumption 48, 50, 51, 57–8; knowledge about alcohol 51, 88–9; quantity of consumption 49, 50, 51; reasons for consumption 51–2; tobacco use 52–3, 58
manual for teachers 65–7, 73, 98
Marsh, A. 11, 22, 38, 54–5, 57, 58, 85
materials, quality 81, 98
meaning-maker, person as 63
media messages 9, 68, 97
method, design 33–5; alcohol education package 61, 63–4
methodology, evaluation 96
Mexico, alcohol consumption 4
Milgram, G. 25
model, defined 13
Monarca, S. 102
Morgan, M. 13

Naidoo, J. 16
needs, assessment 61
Netherlands, alcohol consumption 4
New Zealand, alcohol consumption 4
Nigeria, alcohol consumption 4
North Karelia Youth Project, Finland 26
Norway, tobacco education 22

O'Connor, J. 9–10, 56
Olafsdottir, H. 56
Ontario, Canada cannabis education 22–3; curriculum 101, 105; Ministry of Health 101
Osman, L. 22

parental attitudes: to alcohol consumption 11, 46, 68; and tobacco education 22
patterns of alcohol consumption 1, 6
Peck, D.F. 8
peer group pressure 10, 11, 68, 97
peer-led discussion, effectiveness 21
Pernanen, K. 38
personal construct theory 63, 64, 79

Personal and Social Education curriculum 62
person-oriented approach to drug education 23, 27
Peru, alcohol consumption 4
Perugia, University of 102
Petersen, A. 28
Philippines, alcohol consumption 4
pilot study 32–3
Pitman, D. 5
Plant, M.A. xiv, 8, 11, 20, 26, 28, 31–2, 38, 42, 54, 58, 85, 93
PLUS programme, Canada 101, 105
Poland, alcohol consumption 4
Pope, M. 63
Portugal, alcohol consumption 4
Positive Life Using Skills (PLUS) programme 101, 105
Power, C. 28
pre- and post-intervention measures 20
prevention: primary xv, xvi, 31; secondary xv
preventive education, effectiveness 20–8
primary prevention xv, xvi, 31
'problem behaviour theory' 12–13, 63
problem drinkers, intervention amongst 6
problems, alcohol-related 5; policy responses to 5–6
problem-solving ability 73–4
Promoting Good Health – Proposals for Action 107
psychoactive substance misuse: influences on 12–13, 14; reasons for 7–12
psychoactive substance misuse education xiv; approach adopted 23, 26–7; effectiveness 13–14, 21; and increased use 23, 25, 27, 80; low priority 106
pupils: feedback 77–80, 98; participation 63, 79

questionnaire (Appendix 1a) 38, 41, 109–59; administration 39;

Feedback Forms and 98; Lothian region study 38; Welsh language version 135–59; wording 55
quiz 68–9, 86–7

Rachal, J. 10
reasons for alcohol consumption 7–12
reproduction, high-gloss 70, 77
resource materials *see* materials
responsibility, developing 59
Ritson, B. 8–9
road traffic accidents 11
role-playing: effectiveness 21; in tobacco education 21
Romania, alcohol consumption 4
Rotterdam, drug education programmes 23
Royal College of General Practitioners Report (1986) 5
Royal College of Physicians, Report (1987) 5
Royal College of Psychiatrists 8, 66
Russell, J. 16, 17

Sales, J. 8
Salmon, P. 63
Samuel, E. 31
Scandinavia: alcohol, controls on 103–4; alcohol education xvi; temperance movement 105
scapegoating 7
Schaps, E. 20
school-based alcohol education xv–xvi
Schools Council xv, 60, 61
schools, selection of 35–8
Schurman, J.H. 23
science curriculum, alcohol education in 62
Scotland: age and abstinence 54–5; alcohol education 107; education system 62, 106; frequency of consumption 57; Health Studies 107; parental influence 10; younger children and alcohol 97
Scottish Consultative Council on the Curriculum 107

Scottish Health Education Group xv, 69
secondary prevention xv
Secondary Science Curriculum Review 63
self-confidence 97
self-empowerment 17–18
self-esteem 18, 21, 97
self-reported data 38
seven-day diary 42
sex differences in alcohol use 48–54
skills *see* social skills; life skills
slide material 72, 75
small group work 63, 68, 76–7
Smart, R. 22, 24
smoking 21–2, 47–8; decline 21–2; sex differences 58; acceptability 19
social education, alcohol education in 62, 66, 97
social pressures: in alcohol consumption 8–10; approach 26–7, 96; awareness of 68; and smoking 19, 21
social skills 18, 26, 97
society and alcohol 1, 6, 8–10
South Africa, alcohol consumption 4
Soviet Union (USSR), alcohol consumption 4
Spain, alcohol consumption 4; alcohol education 103; preventive measures 102–3
specialist intervention schools 37
specialist teachers 71–2, 97; feedback from 72–5
spirits, British consumption of 2, 3
Spring, J. 2
Stacey, B. 10
staffing, alcohol education package 62, 65, 97
statistical analyses, evaluation study 160–1
stereotypes of addiction 7
story completion 68
Stuart, R. 24, 25
study areas 33
study group 37, 41–2; age of initiation 56; alcohol education

46–7; attitudes about alcohol 46, 52; developmental stage 64; divisions 84; experience of alcohol 42–4, 48–52, 84, 85–6; ill-effects of alcohol 45; knowledge about alcohol 44–5; selection 41–2, 54–5, 64–5, 66; sex differences 48–54, 57–8; tobacco and illicit drugs 47, 52–4
substance misuse *see* psychoactive substance misuse
survey instrument 38
Sweden: alcohol consumption 4; alcohol education 104–6; context of initiation 56
Swedish Alcohol Retailing Monopoly (Systembolaget) 103–4
Swisher, J.D. 25
Switzerland, alcohol consumption 4
Systembolaget, Sweden 103–4

Taiwan, alcohol consumption 4
target group: age-group selection 66: definition 96; developmental stage 62
target population 62, 64–5
teacher effect 72, 97
teachers 65; Advisory Council on Alcohol and Drug Education xv, 69; alcohol education 32; feedback 72–7, 98; manual for 65–7, 73, 98; restrictions on 76, 81, 97; specialist 71–5, 97
teaching package *see* alcohol education package
television drama, portrayal of alcohol 9
Tether, P. 5, 6
Thompson, J. 101, 102
time, shortage of 75, 77, 81
tobacco use 47–8; decline 21–2; and drug use 47, 52–4, 59; sex differences 58
tobacco education: effectiveness 19, 21–2; parental participation 22; skills-based approach 26
Tones, K. 14, 17–18, 26
topic-centred content 64

topics, possible 74
Transport and Road Research Laboratory xv
Triandis, H.C. 13
Turkey, alcohol consumption 4

under-age drinking 11–12
unemployment and alcohol use 8
United Kingdom: age and abstinence 55, 56; alcohol consumption 1–7; alcohol education xv, 100; future developments 106–8; gender and alcohol consumption 11; real price of alcohol 2, 8; smoking, decline 21–2; tobacco education 22; *Young People and Alcohol* report (1986) 11–12
United States: age and abstinence 55, 56; age of initiation 57; alcohol consumption 4; alcohol education xvi, 100; costs of alcohol misuse 5; drug education 21; frequency of consumption 57–8; gender and alcohol consumption 11, 57–8; National Institute on Alcohol Abuse and Alcoholism 5; parental influence 10; sex differences 57–8
USSR *see* Soviet Union

Vartiainen, E. 26
vehicle offences 11
Venezuela, alcohol consumption 4
victim blaming 16, 61
video, use of 73, 75, 76, 77, 81, 98; effectiveness 21; in tobacco education 21
visual aids 77

Wales, alternative health education campaign 87, 90, 91
warning approach to drug education 23, 25
Welsh language questionnaire (Appendix 1b) 38, 39, 41, 135–59
whole person approach to health education 29

Wilcox, B. 26
wines, British consumption of 2, 3–4
Winton, M. 8
World Health Organization 18–19, 60

Young People and Alcohol report (1986) 11–12
Your Health and Alcohol 101, 105

youth: and advertisements 9; gender and consumption 10–11; peer-group pressure 10; social influences on 9–10; susceptibility 12; under-age drinking 11–12; *see also* adolescence
Yugoslavia, alcohol consumption 4

Zaire, alcohol consumption 4